The highs, the lows...

Canada
Cup '81

81
CANADA CUP
COUPE CANADA

© 1981 Hockey Canada
mark/marque Hockey Canada

PRINTED AND BOUND IN CANADA

ISBN: 0-919035-11-6

Executive Sport Publications Ltd.
15608 - 116 Avenue
Edmonton, Alberta, Canada
T5M 3S5

ACKNOWLEDGEMENTS

"The Highs... The Lows... Canada Cup 1981" is an impressive undertaking involving top photography simultaneously in several cities and a mountain of information from many games. The production of this book is a credit to the hard work and long hours of many individuals. I would like to make special mention to Mr. Rick Pape, the designer of the book, for his extra effort in putting it all together within our deadlines.

The various companies involved also deserve mention for their part in meeting deadlines with super quality:

Lars-Sons Graphics — Stripping
Set Rite Typesetting — Typesetting
Colorgraphics — Color Separations
Stuart-Brandle Printers — Printing
Tritradesmen Bindery — Folding and Collating
Universal Book Bindery — Binding

Finally, I would like to thank The Hudson's Bay Company for their belief in the project and in particular Rod Hooktwith and George Rogers of The Bay for their help in this our newest publication in our growing list of quality sport books.

William F. Dowbiggin
Managing Director
Executive Sport Publications Ltd.

The Authors

Brian McFarlane

Brian McFarlane has been a television commentator for 25 years and has written 15 books on hockey. He is a former All-American hockey player at St. Lawrence University in Canton, N.Y. and is Dean of the Scotiabank Hockey College. He still plays regularly for the NHL Oldtimers.

George Hanson

George Hanson followed a sport journalist career for 26 years, he is currently a freelance-writer-consultant. His writing and consulting talents have been called upon for both national and international events. Mr. Hanson was co-author for the Official Record of the 1976 Innsbruck Winter Olympics and English-Language author for the Official Record on the 1976 Olympic Games, Montreal. He has covered Grey Cup, Stanley Cup and World Series games.

The Photographers

Dave Bonner

Dave Bonner is a freelance photographer based in Winnipeg. He has worked for the Winnipeg Free Press and the Winnipeg Trib Magazine. He has covered Pan Am and Commonwealth games.

Bill Brennan

Bill Brennan is a prominent figure among media photographers in Canada. He has worked for The Ottawa Journal, The Ottawa Citizen, Canadian Press and United Press International in a career highlighted by numerous awards. His feature photos have appeared in major magazines in Canada and the United States — with some magazines such as People commissioning a major work on one of his more controversial subjects, Margaret Trudeau.

The selection of photographers and coverage logistics to produce the photographs for Canada Cup '81 was the work of two professional photo editors. The 10,000 photographs taken of the Canada Cup series were edited, cropped and arranged by David M. Reidie of Edmonton and Peter Robertson of Toronto. Robertson and Reidie bring the experience of many years of editing visual material of major international sporting events to Canada Cup '81. Their selection and arrangement of photographs show the story of Canada Cup '81.

Denis Brodeur

Denis Brodeur is a freelance photographer who has worked in Montreal for many years. His love of hockey stems from having been a goal-tender, and once took over from the renowned Jacques Plante in net. His ability is quite obvious from his superb timing of peak action. He has the respect of the total Montreal Canadiens organization and has the run of the Forum.

Murray Mosher

Murray Mosher is Photo Features of Ottawa. Murray has well earned his reputation of being one of the best news photographers on Capitol Hill, and has been the stringer for the Toronto Star since 1967.

Paul Taillfer

Paul Taillfer is another well-respected Quebec photographer. He was Chief Photographer at the Montreal Star for many years until it folded recently. He is now teaching and running a business including freelance photography.

Team Canada/8
Foreword/11

Team Canada

Row I
M. Lessard
D. Edwards
G. Lafleur
G. Perreault
S. Bowman
I. Grundman
A. Eagleson
C. Fletcher
S. Pollock
D. Sittler
M. Dionne
W. Smith
M. Liut

Row II
E. Palchak
W. Barber
B. Trottier
M. Bossy
J. Gregory
P. Page
Y. Belange
A. MacNeil
G. Berenson
D. Potvin
R. Gainey
L. Robinson
G. Lefebvre
A. Kukulowicz

Row III
B. Engblom
R. Goring
R. Carlyle
D. Gare
Dr. C. Bull
Dr. D. Mackesy
G. Fuller
Dr. D. Kinnear
Dr. S. McGrail
S. Payne
M. Gartner
R. Ramage
C. Gillies
R. Dawe

Row IV
S. Simpson
K. Linsman
D. Taylor
W. Gretzky
P. Coffey
B. Beck
R. Duguay
R. Smith
P. Reinhart
R. Middleton
S. Shutt
R. Bourque
C. Hartsburg
J. Schoenfeld

Photography by James Lipa

Hockey Canada was formed in 1969 to create the opportunity for Canada's best hockey players to play the best hockey players from any other country in the world.

This goal was reached for the first time in 1972 when Hockey Canada negotiated with the Soviet Union for a series of 8 games between Russia's national team and Canada's best professional hockey players. The 1972 Canada-Soviet series was an historic sports event. All of us remember the disappointing loss in the first game in Montreal and all of us remember clearly with pride and excitement Paul Henderson's goal on September 28, 1972, when Canada won the series.

The 1976 Canada Cup was the next step forward for international hockey. The national teams from Canada, the Soviet Union, Finland, Sweden, Czechoslovakia and the United States played a round robin tournament which was full of excitement and surprises. Czechoslovakia defeated Canada, Sweden defeated Czechoslovakia, Finland defeated Sweden, Czechoslovakia defeated Russia and Canada defeated Russia. Canada won the two out of three final series on Darryl Sittler's overtime goal in the second game. The Canada Cup tradition was created with that series and negotiations commenced on the conclusion of the 1976 Canada Cup for the second Canada Cup.

Plans moved ahead and all of the countries were committed to participate in 1980. The timing seemed to be perfect. The Winter Olympics held in Lake Placid resulted in a major upset when United States defeated the Soviet Union and won the gold medal.

The boycott of the 1980 Summer Olympics made it impossible for Hockey Canada to pursue its 1980 Canada Cup program and the Canada Cup was postponed until 1981.

With the support of the Board of Hockey Canada I was able to negotiate the final contract for the Canada Cup of Hockey 1981 in Frankfurt, in January, 1981. This agreement was subject to certain conditions which had to be resolved on or before May 15, 1981. Those conditions included an assurance that proper television sponsorship would be arranged by Canada which would result in sufficient funds being available to the participating countries for their continuing hockey programs.

In the summer of 1981 I was able to work with Harcom Consultants and Mr. Arthur Harnett to finalize the sale of television and board advertising rights which gave Hockey Canada the impetus which permitted it to organize the Canada Cup of Hockey 1981.

The series was exciting from start to finish. Canada finished first in the round robin, the Soviets finished second, Czechoslovakia third and the United States fourth.

The semi-finals played to sell-out crowds. In Ottawa, the Soviets defeated Czechoslovakia, and in Montreal, Canada defeated the United States. This left the final game as a confrontation between the Soviet Union and Canada.

The final game was won by the Soviets 8-1. The score was not indicative of the play because Canada outshot the Soviet Union. During the first period alone Canada could easily have scored several goals had it not been for the brilliant netminding of Vladislav Tretiak. The Soviets took a 3-1 lead in the second period and scored 5 unanswered goals in the third period to win the Canada Cup.

The Canada Cup of Hockey 1981 was an overwhelming success and hockey fans around the world are already looking forward to the Canada Cup of Hockey 1984.

R. Alan Eagleson

1

A Canada Cup
History:
Canada Wins
In '76

The 1975-76 hockey season was a memorable one for Darryl Sittler, captain of the Toronto Maple Leafs. There were nights of unparalleled excellence on the ice, culminating in an overtime goal at the Montreal Forum that swept Team Canada to a stirring victory over the gritty Czechs in the original Canada Cup.

Earlier that year, there were other once-in-a-lifetime accomplishments for Sittler — an astonishing ten points in one game against the Boston Bruins and a record-tying five goal outburst against Philadelphia in a playoff game.

The Canada Cup winning goal was particularly meaningful. It brought Sittler something he'd never experienced with his own team the Leafs — the thrill of winning a championship. In the summer of 1981, Sittler's hopes for a similar thrill soared when he was selected once again for Team Canada. If it hurt to know he was the last player selected, almost as an afterthought, he never let on. There he was battling younger, speedier players for a spot on the roster. He worked desperately hard knowing at age 31 it would be his last chance to represent his country at such a level of competition. He hoped deep inside that his dedication would pay off, possibly in the kind of performance that would equal his spectacular contribution in '76.

But it was not to be. Players were scrutinized, cuts were made. On August 26, following an exhibition game with Team USA Sittler received the depressing news. He was being dropped from the squad. His chance was gone. There would be no opportunity to duplicate the heroics of five years earlier.

Other players cut from the '81 squad such as Paul Coffey, Bobby Smith, and Steve Payne could count on future action against the best from other nations. But Sittler, like other heroes of '76, superstars of international play like Bobby Clarke and Rogie Vachon would have to step back a pace and settle for memories of yesterday's glory.

The recollection of those golden days in '76 would bring a smile of satisfaction to any of the above faces but especially to Sittler's whose goal brought the original Canada Cup to a smashing conclusion.

What grand memories there are. Not only for Sittler and his mates, but for hockey fans everywhere.

There never would have been a Canada Cup but for the steady resolve and determination of Alan Eagleson, Executive Director of the National Hockey League Players Assocation.

In 1969, Eagleson told the world hockey powers he wished to organize an international series, one between the best Canadian pros and the best teams representing the top European nations. Eagleson, a director of newly-established Hockey Canada, was weary of seeing Canadian teams unable to use NHL players, humbled in world Olympic competition. The year he initiated his quest toward a Canada Cup of hockey was the year Canada lost to the Soviets, the Czechs and the Swedes in the world championships and managed to beat only the Finns and the United States. It was in a word, humiliating.

With the 1970 world championships scheduled for Montreal and Winnipeg, Canada proposed that the competition be opened to pros. The proposal was quickly defeated by members of the International Ice Hockey Federation. The IIHF did however, agree to the use of nine pro players, providing they were not employed in the NHL. Then, in a sudden reversal caused by the fear that playing against pros might make all participants ineligible for future Olympic play, the IIHF said no to the pros, touching off angry exchanges among the overseas decision-makers and Hockey Canada officials. Canada opted out of world play, slammed the door on the Europeans and cancelled the 1970 tournament. Canada also banned any Canadian teams of any age from competing abroad.

For two years there was a freeze on international play involving Canadian teams. Finally, after the 1972 Olympics (won by the Soviets), a delegation from Moscow invited Hockey Canada officials to a meeting in Prague. Out of this meeting came plans for an eight-game "friendly" series pitting the Soviet national team against the best players from the NHL.

That series, featuring a remarkable comeback by Team Canada in Moscow, a near-arrest of Alan Eagleson and his subsequent rescue by Team Canada players, a cry for fan support from Phil Esposito on national TV, the defection of several Team Canada "subs" and an incredible last-minute goal by Paul Henderson, was spectacularly successful. The Soviets proved they could keep pace with Canada's best and in exhibition games scheduled around the series, so did the Swedes and the Czechs. Eaglesons call for a world cup of hockey began to make sense to a few million people.

Another summit series was played in 1974, this time between the Soviets and an all-star team from the World Hockey Association. The Soviet players spent much of their time

Gordie Howe vs. Tretiak in the 1974 Canada-Russia Series.

gawking at the legendary Gordie Howe, age 49, and much of their time casting anxious glances at Bobby Hull, another aging superstar. In between times, the Soviets scored often enough to win the series.

Now there was a real clamor for more such confrontations. Other nations wanted in, eager to challenge the two major hockey powers.

In May, 1975, Canada's Health Minister Marc Lalonde announced plans for Canada Cup '76. He introduced Alan Eagleson as chairman of the event. The competing countries would be Canada, Russia, Czechoslovakia, Sweden, Finland and the United States.

Eagleson, a shrewd marketing man, brought huge profits to Hockey Canada and the player's pension plan through the sale of television rights. He arranged for NHL player participation by inserting clauses in the standard player's NHL contract allowing a player to represent his country in international play. He helped persuade his old adversary, Bunny Ahearne, President of the IIHF, to move that pros be allowed to compete in world competitions and he supported Canada's return to the official world championships, using professional players in 1977.

It was only natural that Sam Pollock, Montreal Canadiens' General Manager, would be asked to assemble Canada's entry in the tournament, which would run from Sept. 2 through Sept. 17. Pollock was renowned throughout the hockey world as a builder of champions.

Pollock quickly appointed four coaches instead of the traditional one or two — Scotty Bowman of Montreal, Don Cherry of Boston, Bobby Kromm of WHA Winnipeg Jets, and Al MacNeil of the Nova Scotia Voyageurs. All but Cherry had been with cup-winning teams earlier in the year. Keith Allen of the Philadelphia Flyers was asked to serve as GM of Team Canada and former stars Toe Blake, Gordie Howe, Jean Beliveau and Syl Apps were named as special advisors.

In choosing his players, Pollock selected seven members of his Stanley-Cup winning Montreal Canadiens. They were goalie Ken Dryden, defensemen Serge Savard, Guy Lapointe, and Larry Robinson, forwards Steve Shutt, Pete Mahovlich and Guy Lafleur. He picked three complete lines for the team, including his Montreal trio of Shutt-Mahovlich-Lafleur. From Philadelphia he selected Bobby Clark, Reg Leach and Bill Barber and from Buffalo he chose the famous French Connection of Rene Robert, Gilbert Perreault and Richard Martin. Philadelphia also contributed goalie Bernie Parent and defenseman Jim Watson while Buffalo sent forward Danny Gare.

Others named to the original roster included goalies Gerry Cheevers, Boston, Glenn Resch, Islanders and Rogie Vachon, Los Angeles. Other defensemen were Denis Potvin, Islanders, Carol Vadnais, Rangers, Dave Burrows, Pittsburgh, Paul Shmyr of Cleveland. Other forwards were Phil Esposito, Rangers, Marcel Dionne, Los Angeles, Darryl Sittler and Lanny McDonald, Toronto, Dan Maloney, Detroit and Jean Pronovost, Pittsburgh.

Brad Park of Boston and high-scoring Marc Tardif of Quebec (WHA) were unavailable because of injuries. Bernie Parent and Jim Schoenfeld were ruled out for the same reason and Bobby Orr, recovering from knee surgery, was not expected to play. How could Orr, now minus all the cartilage in one of his troubled knees, possibly be ready in time to suit up against the best players on the planet?

Early in training camp, the veteran players moved quickly to head off any recurrence of the 1972 series when disputes and dissension swept through the team. It was recalled that Gilbert Perreault, Richard Martin, Jocelyn Guevremont and Vic Hadfield deserted the team, claiming they weren't getting enough ice time.

Phil Esposito and Bobby Clarke addressed the team and bluntly

stated that anyone who didn't like the way things were being handled should get out now, not after the tournament got underway.

Esposito said, "It's essential we unite now in an effort to win. Some guys are going to be cut from this team and it's going to hurt. But we've got to put egos aside and accept the decisions of the coaching staff. I'm prepared right now to be cut in training camp. I hope all the other guys feel the same way."

Bobby Hull added, "We're playing for our hockey lives in this one and we'd better be up for it."

Team Canada got a big lift when Bobby Orr checked into camp a few days later. "My legs feel pretty good," he said. "I've been doing knee exercises and I hope I'll be lucky enough to make this team."

Lucky is how the coaches felt, just having Orr on the ice, even though his mobility was hampered by his aching underpinning.

Not so lucky were the players dropped on September 1, the date when the final roster was named. Rene Robert, a 35-goal socrer with Buffalo, Jean Pronovost, a 52-goal shooter with Pittsburgh, WHA all-star defenseman Paul Shmyr, defenseman Dave Burrows of Pittsburgh and hardrock forward Dan Maloney of Detroit were lopped from the squad.

Team Canada was ready, eager to face the Finns in the opening game the following night in Ottawa.

Other teams appeared to be equally well-prepared although some strange decisions in the Soviet camp puzzled North American experts. Familiar stars like Valeri Kharlamov, Aleksandr Yakushev, possibly hockey's best left winger, and others like Vladimir Shadrin, Vladimir Petrov and Boris Mikhailev, were replaced by younger, less famous players.

Kharlomov, the brilliant forward who dazzled Team Canada in the '72 series, was lost to the Soviet club after breaking both ankles in a car accident. There were new coaches as well, a change dictated after a

Bobby Hull in Canada Cup I.

humiliating loss to Poland in the world hockey championships. Boris Kulagin and Konstantin Loktev were given scouting assignments and replaced by Victor Tikchonov and Boris Mayorov.

Of the changes, Harry Sinden said, "When it comes right down to it, the Soviets will show up with a very experienced team. The new kids they are bringing along aren't going to hurt them."

One of those new kids was Helmut Balderis, a Latvian, who was highly praised for his efforts in the world competition. Possessing a powerful shot and great speed, Balderis was said to be a superstar of the future.

Still, the Czechs were considered to be the top threat to the Canadians. Czechoslovakia, beaten by the Soviets 4-3 for the gold medal at the Winter Olympics, reversed the score with a win and a tie against the Soviets at the World Tournament in Poland. They relied heavily on Jiri Holocek in goal, rated as the top European netminder.

If the Czechs missed Vaclav Nedomansky, who defected two years earlier to the Toronto Toros of the WHA, they weren't saying. They still had Milan Novy, the Bobby Clarke of European hockey, and a full roster of stars including Jiri Bubla, Ivan Hlinka, Vladimir Martinec and a rookie named Peter Stastny, of whom great things were expected. The Czech coaches were Karel Gut and Jan Starsi.

The Swedish entry was rated as the dark horse of the competition, one that could move right to the top. On the roster were no less than ten professional players, four from the NHL and six from the WHA. With defenders like Borje Salming and Lars Eric Sjoberg, along with forwards like Anders Hedberg, Ulf Nilsson, Willy Lindstrom, Roland Erickson (leading scorer at the recent World Tournament), Juha Widing and Dan Labraaten, the Swedes could not be treated lightly.

Spoiler roles were handed the U.S. club and the Finns. Team USA,

coached by Bob Pulford of the L.A. Kings, represented the first all American professional hockey team. Despite the fact the Americans boasted a roster of NHL and WHA players they weren't expected to finish in the top four.

The first game in the 1976 Canada Cup tournament — Canada versus Finland — was played in the Ottawa Civic Centre on September 2. It was obvious in the opening moments that the Finns couldn't keep pace with the swift Canadians. Richard Martin scored a power play goal at 3:54 of the first period. Team Canada followed up with three more quick goals, two by Hull and one by Esposito. Antti Leppanen was replaced in goal by young Marcus Mattson but the pressure continued. Martin scored twice in the third period to finish the night with three goals and two assists in an 11-2 romp. Hull and Esposito both clicked for a pair of goals while Sittler, Leach, Perreault and Shutt had the others.

It was a good test for Bobby Orr's tender knee, which stood up to some stiff checks. Orr's defense partner, Denis Potvin, called the game "monotonous." Potvin kept a diary of the tournament. In it he wrote: "I found it difficult to adjust, playing with Orr. Neither of us knew what the hell we were doing so I concentrated on letting him carry the puck and me playing my position. We still didn't play as a disciplined unit."

Potvin was upset when Scotty Bowman did not start him in the opener. He wrote: "Scotty didn't start me in Ottawa and that upset me. Guy Lafleur played junior hockey in Quebec and when we went there to play he was introduced and got a standing ovation. And they gave him his sweater number 4 and they retired it forever. Scotty did the right thing and had Guy start the game and the fans cheered and cheered because they remembered all he did and loved him for it. But Scotty didn't start me and it hurt. In Montreal, he started five Montreal players and I know, in Toronto, he'll start McDonald and Sittler, and so

he should. Even when I was on the ice, there was no recognition from the fans, nothing to say they appreciated my six years on the same rink as a junior."

On September 3, at Maple Leaf Gardens in Toronto, Sweden beat Team USA 5 - 2. Borje Salming paced the Swedes with a goal and an assist. A number of bad penalties in the first period hurt the American chances. The Swedes took full advantage of their power play opportunities and collected four of their five first period goals while holding the man advantage.

On the same day, in Montreal, the Czechs were in top form against the Soviets and skated off with an impressive 5-3 victory. Midway through the first period, playing with a man advantage, the Czech captain Pospisil raced down the left side, timed a perfect pass to Milan Novy who whipped a shot at Tretiak in the Soviet goal. Tretiak stopped the shot but Novy pounced on the rebound and slipped it into the net. Pospisil made it 2-0 Czechoslovakia in the final minute of the first period.

Again in the second period, the Soviets gave up a goal with only seconds to play. It gave the Czechs a 3-1 lead and just the sort of boost they needed to foil some frantic Soviet rushes in the third. Canadian fans marvelled at the discipline displayed by both clubs during the match. The Czechs went offside only three times and the Soviets just twice. In NHL play, there are an average of 25 offsides per game.

"We'll get better," promised one of the Soviet coaches after the match. "Our team is still developing and we have many new faces. The Czechs have a strong team but remember, they have been together for a very long time."

Two days later, it was Sweden's turn to keep the Soviets off the win sheet. With less than three minutes to play and Sweden trailing 3-2, Anders Hedberg took a quick pass from Borje Salming and raced in on Soviet goaltender Vladislav Tretiak. Hedberg's rising shot eluded Tretiak, the shot that tied the game 3-3. Hedberg's dance of joy ended abruptly when his teammates barrelled into him, eager to show their appreciation.

The Soviets, after only two games, were perilously close to missing any chance at winning the cup.

"We're getting better," said Tretiak. "It's disappointing to play so well and still not win."

In Toronto that night, fans who came to see the goaltending style of Jiri Holocek didn't get much of a chance to study the man billed as "Europe's best goalie". Holocek was called upon to make only 15 saves as Czechoslovakia humiliated Finland 8-0. Still, goaltending was the story of the game, as Finland's Antti Leppanen faced 40 shots and made some incredible saves.

"I envied Holocek at the other end of the ice," said Leppanen at game's end. "He had a very easy time and I thought how nice it would be to change nets with him. Still, I like to face lots of shots. It lets me know I'm in the game from start to finish."

In exhibition play prior to the tournament, Team Canada scored two easy victories over Team USA. But on September 5 at the Montreal Forum the Americans threw a real scare into their northern neighbours. There was no reason to fear an upset in the first period as Phil Esposito. Pete Mahovlich and Bobby Hull opened up a 3-0 lead for Team Canada. Again it was a case of the Americans taking too many penalties as two of the first three goals were power play scores.

Instead of folding, as many suspected they would, the Americans stormed out in the second period and scored twice to narrow the margin to 3-2. Now the Canadians realized they were in a battle. In the third, Team USA kept the pressure on and missed the tying goal on several occasions. Then with a minute left in the game, Bob Pulford pulled his goalie in favour of an extra attacker. But Darryl Sittler snared the puck with 13 seconds on

the clock and fired it into the open net from a sharp angle to give Team Canada a 4-2 victory.

Pete LoPresti was the biggest star for Team USA, stopping 32 of 35 shots. Rogie Vachon, in goal for Team Canada, faced only 16 shots.

"One more shot and they might have tied it," smiled Vachon. "They showed a lot of determination and drive."

Team Canada defenseman Jim Watson suffered a serious injury in the game. Watson was knocked down by a Gary Sargent slapshot and suffered broken bones above and below his left eye.

Poor Finland. They tried so hard against the Soviets in a game at the Forum on September 7, and still lost 11-3.

Viktor Zhluktov, a 22-year-old giant forward on the Soviet team, more than any other player, was responsible for the drubbing. Zhluktov, with a long stride and a reach to match, collected four goals against the Finns and helped set up two more by Alexsandr Vikulov. Brodie Snyder, a veteran hockey writer, was impressed with the Finns never-give-up attitude. He wrote: "It was heartbreaking to see them consoling each other after another one-sided beating . . . far from home, out of their league, very young."

On the same evening in Toronto, Borje Salming of Sweden won a tremendous ovation when he was introduced prior to the match with Team Canada. The applause for Salming rankled some members of Team Canada. "It's almost as if Salming and the Swedes are the home team and we're the visitors," said one. The word from the Canadian coaches on Salming was: "Don't let him get started. If he controls the puck he can kill you. Get on him fast — in his own end of the rink."

Sittler stood up in the dressing room and demonstrated Salming's techniques, how he pivoted in his own zone a lot of the time. Sittler told his teammates not to go for Salming's fakes but to skate right into him, knock him off the puck.

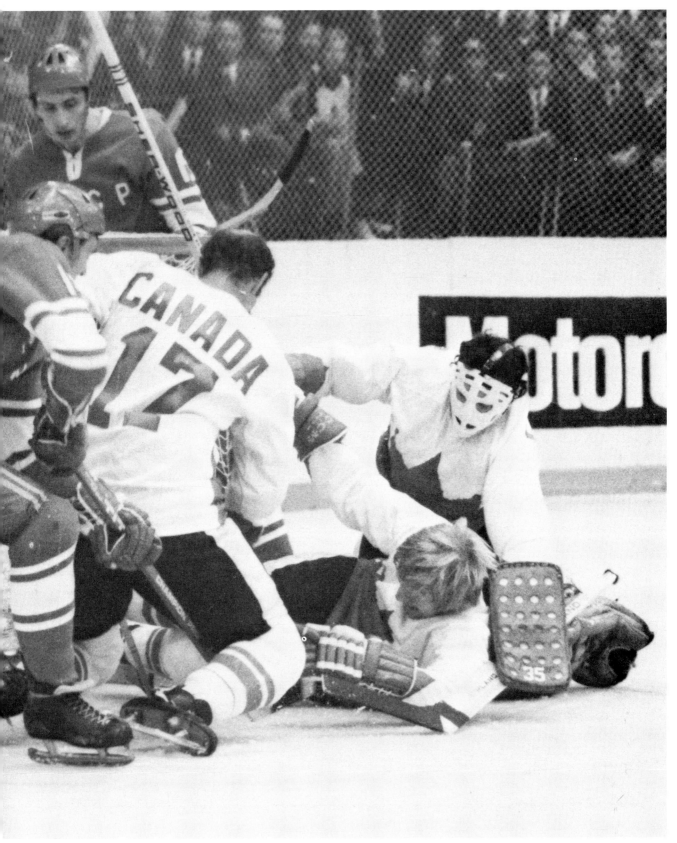

Scramble in front of Canadian Net in '72 Canada-Russian Series.

Phil Esposito being checked in '72 in Canada-Russian Series.

Salming was the recipient of three solid checks early in the game — one by Bill Barber and two by Bobby Hull. The heavy body work slowed him down. Anders Hedberg, meanwhile, was checked to a standstill by Bob Gainey, who neglected his checking chores just often enough to score two goals. Rogie Vachon, whose work in goal continued to be impressive, collected the shutout as Team Canada won 4-0.

A full house of 17,077 turned out at the Spectrum in Philadelphia on Sept. 7 to applaud the USA in a game against the World Champion Czechs. The game turned out to be a thriller. After a scoreless first period, the Americans fell behind 1-0 in the second. Then they exploded for three quick goals and went into the final period leading 4-2. Team USA was 20 minutes away from the biggest upset in the tournament.

Ivan Hlinka, who had scored the first Czech goal, connected again early in the third to make it 4-3. With time running out, Josef Augusta took a shot at goalie Mike Curran. The shot was turned away but the rebound came right out to Augusta. Augusta fell to the ice but the puck, smothered by his body, went into the net with him. The game ended 4-4.

Craig Patrick paced Team USA against the Czechs with two goals while Alan Hangsleben and Robbie Ftorek added one each.

Coach Bob Pulford said of his team's performance, "We played well enough to win. Sometimes a team is simply not rewarded for what it does. This was one of those cases."

On Sept. 9, when the Finns took the ice against Team Sweden in the Winnipeg Arena, they were angry. They felt that people were laughing at them, that they were being dismissed as a team that didn't belong. And they were determined to take out their anger on the Swedes. Team Sweden, on the other hand, was looking forward to a weekend showdown with the Czechs and hopefully, a berth in the finals. Team Sweden coasted to a 4-1 lead over

Finland and then began making costly mistakes. The Finns capitalized every time and closed the gap to 4-3. The Swedes began to reel under the repeated attacks of the Finns. A flurry of goals gave Finland an 8-6 victory, their first of the competition. The fans cheered them now. And the laughter stopped.

At the Spectrum in Philadelphia on Sept. 9, Team USA was unfortunate enough to meet a Soviet team that played flawless hockey. Defenseman Lou Nanne would say after the game, "They were awesome tonight, by far the best team we've met in the tournament so far." The game was a 5-0 shutout for the Soviets. The Soviet line of Viktor Zhluktov, Boris Alexandrov and Vladimir Vikulov did most of the damage. They scored the first four Soviet goals with Alexandrov getting a pair.

The game was rough and Soviet coach Boris Mayorov criticized the American players for their tactics. He accused the American players of trying to provoke the Soviet players into fighting.

At the Montreal Forum that same night, there was a dramatic meeting between the two undefeated teams, Czechoslovakia and Canada. Denis Potvin would describe it later as "one of the finest games ever played at the Forum, they had a system and we still didn't have one."

The fans were captivated by a portly veteran in the Czech goal — Vladimir Dzurilla, who was merely sensational. Dzurilla had replaced the more highly-rated Holocek earlier in the tournament and had outshone his famous countryman. Holocek was turning out to be a flop. Dzurilla didn't use his stick or glove much. He simply threw his body in front of shots, blocking many with his massive chest.

Dzurilla's brilliance in the Czech goal was matched by the acrobatic Rogie Vachon in Team Canada's net. Both men stopped rush after rush and it appeared the game would be decided for overtime. Then, late in the third period, Milan Novy wrestled Sittler for the puck and came up with it. The puck went to Martinec, then over to Augusta. Augusta swung left, taking the Team Canada defenders with him. Novy dashed into the open slot, took Augusta's perfect pass and slammed the puck past Vachon. The games only goal came at 15:41. In the final frantic minutes, Dzurilla was unbeatable even after Vachon was pulled for an extra attacker.

After the game, Potvin wrote: "Now we're in one hell of a mess. If we lose to the Russians on Saturday, we're out of it. We won't even make the playoffs. We must think positive. We are the best and we must believe it and show it."

More than one hockey writer called it, "the battle for the basement" when Team USA met Finland in Montreal on Sept. 11. Both clubs had enjoyed some good moments in the tournament but on the final day they were both right where the experts said they would be, trying to avoid last place.

Throughout the tournament the Americans had been slow starters, giving up two or three goals in the first period. In this game they did it again and fell behind 2-0.

During the first intermission the Americans pulled themselves together. They wanted at least one win in the tournament and this was their final chance to get it. Fred Ahearn scored, then Robbie Ftorek. Mike Milbury scored the go-ahead goal late in the second period and, with only 12 seconds left, Ftorek scored his second goal to give Team USA a 4-2 lead. Bill Nyrop and Mike Polich added third period goals before Pekka Rautakallie knocked the puck past Pete LePresti for the final goal.

Despite the lone victory, the Americans were well-satisfied with their hard-earned tie against the Czechs and the scare they'd given Team Canada.

In Quebec City on Sept. 11, Team Sweden, with no chance of making the finals, wanted to regain some of the price they'd lost in Winnipeg against the Finns. The way to do it was to go out and beat the undefeated Czechs. The Czechs, already assured a berth in the finals, could hardly be faulted if they took the Swedes lightly although team officials promised they'd be playing full out.

A Czech official turned an angry look at a reporter who suggested the Czechs might be coasting. "That's ridiculous," he snorted. "Of course we want to win or tie. Our goal is to finish this tournament in first place and undefeated."

Dzurilla was emerging as one of the top stars of the tournament. He had shutout the USA over one period on Tuesday, then blanked Canada 1-0 on Thursday. Against Sweden, he appeared to be as invincible as ever as he completed the first two periods without allowing a goal. The Czechs, meanwhile took a 1-0 lead on a power play goal by Mar-

Bobby Orr and Phil Esposito in final of Canada Cup in 1976.

tinec. But two penalties late in the period meant the Czechs would be playing two men short to begin play in the third.

Just 31 seconds into the final period, Salming's shot from the point zipped past Dzurilla for the tying goal. A few minutes later, Salming scored another power play goal on a long slapshot that found the corner of the net. The Swedes were able to protect their lead despite some strong pressure from the Czechs. The Czechs finally tasted defeat and the Swedes salvaged a little pride.

All eyes turned to Maple Leaf Gardens in Toronto for the game that night between Team Canada and the Soviets, a game that would decide the Czech's opponent in the finals.

The tension in the Team Canada dressing room before the game with the Soviets was described in one word by Denis Potvin — "awful." Canada had six points, one less than Czechoslovakia and one more than the Soviets. A Soviet win would move them into the finals with the Czechs, a tie would give Team Canada a ticket to the finals.

"To hell with the tie," said Bill Barber. "We've got to win. We've got to beat these guys."

In a surprise move, coach Scotty Bowman benched veteran Phil Esposito and replaced him with Gilbert Perreault. Bowman called it "one of the toughest decisions I've ever had to make in hockey."

Canada scored first on the power play. Perreault tipped Potvin's point shot past Tretiak. The Soviets stormed back and earned the tying goal when Vikulov pounced on a rebound after Vachon had made a big save.

Late in the period, Perreault who played an outstanding game, chased after a loose puck behind Dzurilla's net. He spotted Bobby Hull racing in and threaded a pass to Hull's waiting stick. Hull ripped the puck past Dzurilla and Canada held a 2-1 lead.

In the second, Bill Barber scored the only goal on a tip-in of a Guy Lapointe shot. It was the insurance

goal Team Canada was looking for, and with a number of prolonged ovations to spur them on, Team Canada skated off with a 3-1 victory. There was now only one team between them and the Canada Cup.

Potvin, well-satisfied with his play against the Soviets, was upset when the Player-of-the-Game award went to Bobby Orr.

"I thought I had my best game of the series," he would say. "But when they announced the top player, it went to Bobby Orr. It's hard for me to accept that my best game was not good enough to win it. I feel I was the best player on the ice because of my two assists. And plus one. I'm fair and broad-minded and I look at things pretty logically, I think, but this is something I don't understand and I don't think I ever will."

The memorable series of 1972 between the Soviets and Team Canada resulted in Soviet-style hockey coming under close scrutiny. Canadians wanted to know how the Soviets were able to develop such awesome teams, and so many highly-skilled players, in such a short time span. After all, the Soviets had only been exposed to the game a mere 25 years or so. Books and articles appeared analyzing the Soviet system. Superstars like Yakushev, Tretiak and Kharlamov were profiled on Hockey Night in Canada. These were the men who posed the greatest threat to Canada's claim to hockey's crown.

Little was known of the Czechs. A forward line of centre Milan Novy, 25, and his wingers Vladimir Martinec, 26, and Josef Augusta, 29, might be considered a high-scoring unit by European standards but hardly worth mentioning in the same breath with Boston's famed unit of Esposito, Hodge and Cashman, or Buffalo's flashy threesome of Perreault, Martin, and Robert — the French Connection. NHL scouts and coaches may have spotted the quality in the top forward line of the Czechs, they may have praised others like Peter Stastny, a 19-year-

old newcomer and Milan Chalupa, a defenseman. But for the most part, they remained relatively silent. Like the fans, they waited to be convinced, they wanted to see more.

Certainly they were convinced the Czechs had problems in goal. Jiri Holocek, the man billed as the "best European netminder" had been a major disappointment. Off his play in the tournament, it was unlikely any NHL club would have signed him had he been available. His back up, Vladimir Dzurilla, a gregarious 34-year-old had captured the hearts of Canadians in the manner of a Gump Worsley but only because of one game, the 1-0 thriller over Team Canada. No, it was better to wait and see what the Czechs could do under real pressure before building any pedestals for Novy, Dzurilla or any of the rest.

In retrospect, it was strange the Czechs didn't get more respect. Hockey in Czechoslovakia is older than the country itself. According to George Gross, a former Czech tennis and soccer star, and now sports editor of the Toronto Sun, hockey was introduced to Czech athletes in the early 1900's by students at Oxford, who had learned the game from Canadians. At that time the country was known as Bohemia. Bohemia formed part of a new nation called Czechoslovakia in 1918, after World War I.

"The man who gets most of the credit for the dramatic improvement in Czech hockey," says Gross, "is Mike (Matej) Buckna of Trail, B.C., the son of a Slovak immigrant. In 1935, Buckna travelled overseas and established himself as Europe's outstanding hockey player. Thousands flocked to rinks everywhere he played to admire the skating, stick-handling and hitting talents of this import from Canada."

As a player and coach, Buckna introduced young Czech players into the science of Canadian hockey. Later, as head coach of the Czech Nationals, Buckna guided his proteges to Czechoslovakia's first world title in 1947.

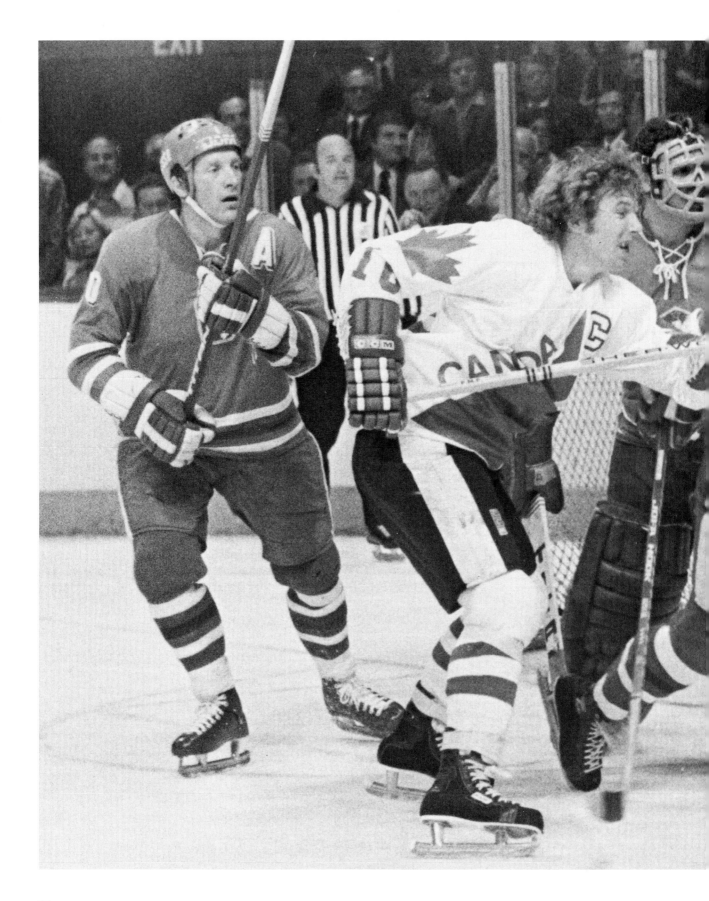

Bobby Clarke: Canada Cup I.

Gross recalls a thrilling Canada-Czech matchup at the 1948 Olympic Games in St. Moritz, Switzerland.

"The Czech team held the powerful RCAF Flyers from Ottawa to a goalless draw thanks to Buckna's clever defensive strategy. However, Czechoslovakia, which won their remaining seven games as, of course, did Canada, had to be satisfied with the silver medal because the Ottawa Flyer's goal average was superior, 69-5, against Czechoslovakia's 80-18.

Buckna's team was back a year later to win the world championship in Stockholm, Sweden, edging Canada in a 1-0 thriller. It was Czechoslovakia's second world title in three years.

Three more world titles followed — in 1972, 1976 and 1977 — to go with a dozen European titles.

In the late 1940's the Czechs helped pass along their winning style to the Soviets, who were then infants at the game, using magazines for shin pads and crude sticks made from tree branches. The first Soviet artificial ice rink was still in the planning stages.

Indeed, Czechoslovakia's reputation as a world hockey power was well established.

Game one of the Canada Cup finals was played at Maple Leaf Gardens on September 13. It was a best-of-three affair and now, with the tournament nearing a climax, millions of fans were caught up in the excitement.

Dzurilla, whose superb play in the earlier 1-0 victory had won him instant celebrity status, was the Czech choice in goal. It didn't take long for Canada to find out his magic had deserted him.

In the opening moments of play, Gilbert Perreault raced down the wing and fired a long shot at Dzurilla. Goal! Right through the pads.

Every team likes a quick start, an early goal. It lifts a team, gives it confidence, erases fear of failure. Perreault's goal had every Canadian player thinking, "We can beat these guys . . . their goalie is only human. Let's pile it on."

Team Canada stormed into the Czech zone and scored three more times before the period ended. Potvin scored the second goal, Orr the third and Lafleur the fourth.

That was all for Dzurilla. Holocek replaced him for the second period and was able to keep his net free of pucks despite some close plays around his goal. In the third, Orr scored again (his second goal and third point of the night) and in the final second of play, Sittler jammed a loose puck past Holocek to give Canada a 6-0 victory.

"We were really well prepared for them," said Bobby Hull, who assisted on Perreault's goal. "In the 1-0 game against them, we did three things poorly. We turned the puck over to them too often, we failed to get two forecheckers into their zone early enough and we failed to cut off their break out play up the middle. We didn't make those mistakes tonight."

With Team Canada coaches warning against over-confidence, the rivals moved on to Montreal and game two at the Forum.

Karel Gut, the Czech coach, was quick to praise Team Canada's effort in game one. "It's obvious they are the best," said Gut. "My players are anxious now to get this tournament finished. They are a long way from home and anxious to get back with their families."

Gut made it sound as if the Czechs were ready to concede. Team Canada members were warned not to be lulled by Gut's purring. One reporter nicknamed him "Cat" Gut and said his psyche job was impressive, right up there with old masters like Imlach, Francis and Blake."

On game day, Gut had more important things on his mind than psychological ploys. He must name a starting goalie. Would it be Holocek or Dzurilla? Dzurilla had stopped Team Canada cold in one game and was playing the best hockey of his career. But Holocek, in recent seasons, was considered to be the Czech's best. Gut opted for Holocek.

Among the more than 18,000 spectators who jammed the Forum that night of Sept. 15 was Prime Minister Pierre Trudeau. The nation's leader, like everybody else, wanted to witness what promised to be one of hockey's greatest moments.

Team Canada hoped to put early pressure on Holocek. And it was Gilbert Perreault who rattled the veteran netminder in the second minute of play. Perreault took a quick pass from Lafleur, zipped around Jiri Bubla, and cruised in on Holocek. Holocek was helpless on Perreault's quick backhand shot and the Forum erupted as Team Canada took a 1-0 lead.

The Czech coaches frowned and turned sour looks on Holocek. But they made no move to replace him.

Seconds later, Potvin lunged for the puck at the point, kept it in the Czech zone and ripped a low shot to the side of the net. Phil Esposito was there to trap it. He whirled and placed the puck expertly behind Holocek. It was 2-0 Canada and only 3:09 had been played.

Holocek was waved to the bench, then directed to the *end* of the bench. On came Dzurilla.

With Dzurilla's bulky form inspiring confidence, the Czechs skated harder, moved the puck out of their own zone with less trouble and survived the period with no more goals against.

Bill Barber's second period penalty paved the way for the Czech's first score. Vachon made three good stops but the penalty killers weren't giving him much help. Machac, from the point, fed the puck to Martinec in the corner. Novy raced in, took Martinec's perfect pass and caught a corner of the net behind Vachon. Canada 2, Czechoslovakia 1.

Midway through the period, Dzurilla made a pair of dazzling saves, first on Orr, then on Esposito.

The Czechs poured into the Canadian zone early in the third period and at 2:14 Puzar's shot tied the score at 2-2. While the Czechs appeared to be gaining momentum Team Canada suddenly ran into

some frustrating moments, setbacks that often demoralize the best of teams. On one play, Hull rapped the puck into the Czech goal but the referee whistled the play dead a split second earlier, having lost sight of the puck.

Hull was right back moments later, hurling his body after a loose puck at the side of the net. He snapped a shot at Dzurilla. Out came a short rebound. Bobby Clarke, ignoring a sore knee and a bruised ankle, leaped in after it and poked the disc past Dzurilla. Canada 3, Czechoslovakia 2.

Now the pace picked up as the teams played some of the most entertaining hockey of the tournament. But the scorers were stymied by stout defensive play and the stubborn efforts of Dzurilla and Vachon.

Then, a whistle. Potvin was penalized at 14:23. The Czechs already owned one power play goal in the game, now they wanted another. But Team Canada's record against the power play throughout the tournament was almost perfect. Until Novy scored earlier in the game, the Canadians had survived 22 situations in which they were short handed. Now the Czechs lined up, hungry for the puck, looking for the tie. Half a minute into the penalty, Machac barged in from the blueline. His shot hit Vachon, trickled off to the side where Augusta was waiting, eager to tap it in. Score tied at three.

Less than a minute later, the Czechs clicked for the go-ahead goal. Bobby Orr went down, injured by a hard shot Orr watched helplessly as Marian Stastny fooled Vachon. Over the boards came the Czech players to pound Stastny on the back. There were exactly four minutes left to play.

The pace quickened even more, there were just over two minutes left when a pair of Philadelphia teammates, Bobby Clarke and Reg Leach, raced up the ice with Barber pushing hard to catch up. Leach, a noted shooter, drove the puck at Dzurilla. The chunky Czech leaped in front

Ken Dryden makes a save in '72.

of the shot but had no control over the rebound. Barber pounced on it, shot and scored. Now it was Canada's turn to celebrate.

Overtime at the Forum, scene of so many dramatic overtime games in the past. But never the setting for overtime in a major international tournament. One player would emerge as the game-winning hero. Who would get the goal and the glory?

There was little chatter in the Team Canada dressing room. The players listened as Don Cherry offered a few words of advice.

"Dzurilla's coming way out of his net on some of our shots," said Cherry. "I tell you, he's got the angles covered pretty well. What I think we should do is hesitate a little bit, that is if a guy is going in alone on him. Let Dzurilla come out. Try to step around the guy. It should give you a heckuva target to shoot at.

And the important thing is to get a couple of good chances early and not let them get any."

When Cherry finished, Lanny McDonald looked over at his close friend Darryl Sittler.

"Okay, Sitt, it's up to you," said McDonald.

Early in the overtime, the puck slipped into the Czech goal but cheers turned to groans when the referee waved the apparent score off.

"The goal net was dislodged just before the puck went in," he ruled.

At the 10 minute mark, again the puck skidded past Dzurilla. More cheers and another judgment.

"Time was out," ruled the ref. Under international rules, the teams changed ends midway through the overtime period.

While the teams changed goals, the fans talked mostly about Vachon and a fabulous save he'd made on

Martinec. The Czech star might easily have ended the game. He was all alone in front of Vachon and slashed a rolling puck upward, aiming for a spot under the crossbar. But Vachon threw up his glove and trapped the puck, kept it out, earned thanks, answered prayers.

Back of the Team Canada bench, Scotty Bowman changed lines quickly. He'd been shuffling his combinations throughout the game and now he called three names. "Sittler, Dionne, McDonald."

The play started innocently enough. McDonald wheeled in his own zone, moved the puck expertly up to Dionne. Dionne spotted Sittler barrelling up the ice and whipped the pass over. Sittler's charge carried him past Chalupa and suddenly the fans sensed it. The big moment was here, the best chance so far. They leaped up as Sittler eluded a desperate dive by Stastny, now there

was just one man to beat . . . the steady Dzurilla.

But Dzurilla was moving . . . charging out to meet Sittler's challenge. Sittler spotted the move, hesitated, recalling the words of Cherry he moved the spinning puck around the pads, past the goal skates, the flailing stick and there it was — a path of clear ice to the open net.

It wasn't a big opening. Just enough and Sittler did not fail. As Dzurilla made a last frantic lunge with his stick and glove, Sittler released his shot. Two steps later he was in behind the Czech goal, arms aloft in the traditional signal of success. The red light confirmed his achievement, the winning goal, the Canada Cup championship.

A flood of red and white jerseys came off the Team Canada bench. They enveloped Sittler, buckling his knees under the weight of their joy. Fans roared their approval and the Prime Minister's applause matched that of the most ardent spectator.

Later Sittler would say, "I remember that moment as one of the happiest of my life. I was so pleased to score but it could just as easily have been Lanny or Marcel who got the goal. I have often thought to myself, what if the puck failed to go in? How terrible I would have felt."

And he would add, "How I admired the Czechs for the graceful way they accepted their defeat. It must have been crushing for them to lose like that in overtime. Had to

be. But they were smiling as they shook our hands and congratulated us. Both teams played tremendous hockey. The Czechs knew they had accomplished much in reaching the finals ahead of the Soviets. The fans gave both teams a standing ovation and there was a strong feeling of mutual respect among the players on both clubs."

When the players lined up along the bluelines for the presentation of awards, the fans shouted their appreciation when Dzurilla was named player-of-the-game for the losers. Dzurilla's ovation was almost as long and loud as that reserved for Sittler, who was named star of the game for Team Canada.

"A unique and wonderful thing

Darryl Sittler's winning goal in Canada Cup I.

happened right after those ceremonies," recalls Sittler. "Suddenly, one player peeled off his hockey sweater and offered it to a player on the other team. Then another did the same thing. Soon we were all tugging off our Team Canada jerseys and pulling on the sweaters of the Czech nationals. It was so right for the moment, such a sporting meaningful gesture and the fans loved it. I traded my sweater with the Czech player Bubla. I still have his sweater at home. I see it there every once in a while and I smile in memory of that memorable night at the Montreal Forum."

Denis Potvin, one of Team Canada's brightest stars, would scribble in his diary, "My senses are still reeling and tumbling . . . that (the final goal) was the sweetest moment of all the moments. It was a precious moment that I wished could have lasted and lasted and never gone away. Lanny looking across at Darryl in the dressing room and saying, "Well, Darryl, I guess it's up to you" because Darryl had scored the final goal in four of our six games — and then actually going out and doing it again for us. I mean, he went out and scored the goddam last goal that made us champions of the whole wide world, that made us and Canada proud. What a great player Sittler is! What a great competitor he was for us."

Potvin would dwell on the moment when Bobby Clarke grabbed a huge Canada flag and skated around the ice with it and how the crowd cheered and waved when all the Team Canada players fell in behind Clarke, skating a couple of victory laps.

"We were all one then, all of us," said Potvin. "The crowd waved and we waved back and when the flag got stuck, I unfurled it because I wanted the whole world to see that we were Canadians and this was *Canada's* victory."

A few weeks later, when Potvin's feelings and thoughts about the Canada Cup were revealed in a national magazine, his refreshing candor brought him criticism, some of his comments about Bobby Orr resulted in some angry fan mail.

"I don't apologize for the things I said and wrote," he said. "They were the things I felt at the time. I'm second to no one in my admiration of Orr as a player and as a man. He's the greatest player of his time and everyone on Team Canada was overjoyed that he could play. He added a great deal to the team, both on the ice and with his attitude."

"It's just that in two games, against the Soviets when we made the finals and the first game of the showdown with the Czechs, I felt I was the top Canadian player. I sincerely felt at the time that I deserved one of those awards. That's not a knock against Orr and the people who see it that way have it wrong. It's more a criticism of the aura that's built up around Orr and the people who put it there."

Most fans, and *all* members of the media, wished there were more men like Potvin, players who were not afraid to display their feelings at the risk of being considered vain or arrogant.

Frank Orr, a respected hockey writer with the *Toronto Star* wrote: "Denis comes across as a remarkably human young man with all the frailties which all hockey players possess but are afraid to show to the world."

Potvin took his readers behind the dressing room door and revealed little habits and personality traits that brought laughter and lightness to a serious occasion.

"One day someone wrapped about 100 feet of black tape around Phil Esposito's shower thongs. Espo is very superstitious and he believed his thongs brought him good luck. He refused to cut the tape because he didn't want to damage the thongs. So he sat there fuming and cursing and unwinding the tape by hand and moaning about how much bad luck this would bring him. Then he went out that night and scored three goals."

"I got to like Guy Lapointe very much and recall him handing a box of cigars to Carol Vadnais, a real cigar mooch. Vadnais opened the

box and got an electric shock. That broke us up."

"I remember other little things the guys did. Bobby Orr tapping each player on the shoulder with his stick just before we took the ice, a little good luck gesture of his. Then there was Guy Lafleur pacing the dressing room floor with barely controlled nerves before each game."

"There was Bobby Hull, 37-years-old playing like a kid. Such a nice guy who liked everybody and was liked by everybody. They call him the Golden Jet and he really is golden, there's such an aura around him."

Hull would remember the Canada Cup for the opportunity it gave him to play with a collection of the

greatest hockey players he'd ever seen. It made up for the hurt and bitterness he felt when he was ignored (as a WHA player) by the selectors who formed Team Canada '72.

"The greatest thing," said Hull, "was that I was able to play with all these fine fellows and especially with Bobby Orr for the first time. Bobby didn't make the opening of training camp. It was a few days before he arrived. Now we had some very fine defensemen on the team but when Bobby showed up and took a few turns on the ice it was like a man playing with boys. He was a marvel. Bobby deserves all the credit he got during his career and it's a shame he was forced to retire early. Just playing with him and just playing with that club was a thrill. There's no question it was the greatest team I ever played on."

"I'll never forget how close I became to being the series hero late in the final game. Guy Lafleur and I broke in alone on Dzurilla. Guy had the puck and made a try for the goal but Dzurilla came up with a big save. All the while I could see that a quick pass to me over on the left side would have caught Dzurilla by surprise. I'm sure I would have scored and the series would have been over. But those things happen all the time in hockey."

"When Darryl scored in overtime, and no better guy could have scored the winner, it was a wonderful moment. Darryl's not only a great player but an outstanding human being. He came up to me after it was all over, after he'd heard that somebody had been telling the kids a bunch of lies about me, and he said 'Bobby, I never make judgments until I know what has gone on myself and I want you to know that it's been a thrill to play with you and to be right there beside you, representing Canada on the same club. It's been terrific.'"

"It was terrific for me too, terrific for all of us."

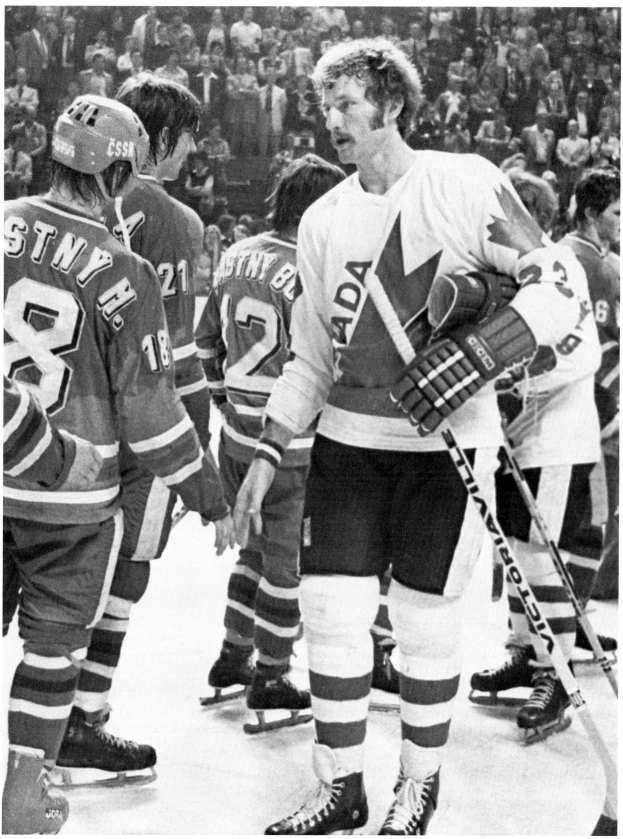

Larry Robinson and Team Canada congratulated by Czechoslovakian team after winning the first Canada Cup.

2

1981 Series:
A Prologue

Concentration by The Great Gretzky.

Reijo Ruotsalainen being watched by Wayne Gretzky.

Wayne Gretzky scores against Finland.

Gilbert Perreault digs the puck out along the boards.

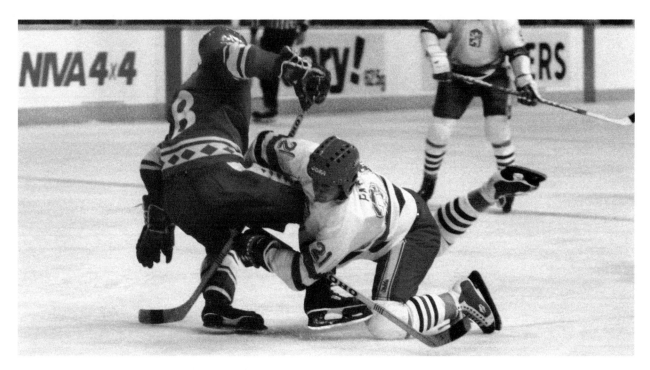

Quiet confidence on the Russian bench.

Dusan Pasek checking Sergei Kapustin

A happy Team Czechoslovakia after their tie with Team USSR.

Richie Dunn stopping Anders Hedberg's rush.

Stefan Persson fights off Mike Ramsey's check.

Swedish fans turned out in Winnipeg.

Canadian fan in Montreal.

Valery Vasiliev takes Bob Gainey into the boards.

Brian Engblom vs. Alexander Skvortsov.

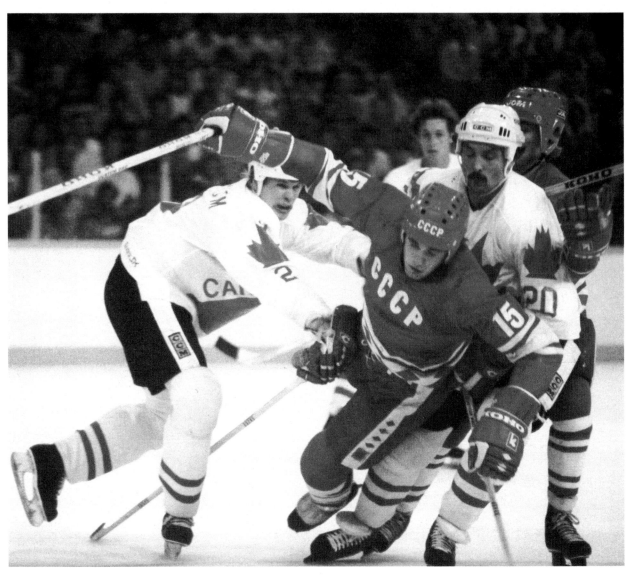

Brian Engblom checks Nikolai Drozdetski with Brian Trottier's help.

Marcel Dionne watching clock in players box.

Sergei Shepelev after Canada's win in Edmonton.

*Team Canada in a happy
moment.*

Valery Vasiliev congratulates a cut Larry Robinson after first Canada-USSR game.

It had come together after almost being stillborn!

It matured through the adolescence of round-robins and semi-finals and then arrived at its brief adulthood in the Montreal Forum on September 13, 1981.

The Canada Cup arrived at what many felt was its raison d'être, a date for all the chips featuring Canada and arch-rival Soviet Union.

It was a sunny day in Montreal, a bonus after 10 days which had stuttered between summer and an unusually early and depressing autumn. Across the land, Canadians were pouring out their gratitude and reverence for a young man named Terry Fox in mini-marathons to raise cancer research money.

In the course of the day, more than 10,000 runners passed by the Forum as part of the giant Montreal International Marathon . . . . not part of the Fox run but a classic in the world of 26 mile 385 yarders.

Leading into this confrontation which was to assuage years of torment and uncertainty concerning whether or not we were, and are, kings of the hockey hill, other news events gained less than their normal headline attention.

Montreal, the point of the arrow as the tournament moved to the stages people wanted, had what normally would be magnified traumas: Dick Williams was fired as Expos coach and, the day before the Canada Cup final, the Alouette' record dropped to 1-9 and Joe Scanella was pink-slipped. The groundswell for each was strong but nothing compared to what it would have been had sports pages and sportscasts not been preoccupied with this hockey event which never fails to bring out the emotional best and worst in Canadians.

Scotty Bowman, head coach of the group coaching what was considered the most skillful assortment of Canadians ever assembled for hockey, believes in portents and omens. However, he had little to say about the possible pitfalls in the juxtaposition of the team's seventh meaningful game (as opposed to exhibitions) and the 13th day of the month. Probably he felt one cancelled out the other so it evened up in the realm of superstition and the occult.

For Alan Eagleson, the hated and loved tournament organizer who won his spurs while bringing down the wrath of a nation for his 'arms up' signal in 1972, watched the game vowing that this would be his last fling as both czar and maestro of it.

With the difficulties of creating Canada Cup II, Eagleson had been hammering at the point that someone else, private enterprise or even government, should inherit the task and responsibility in the future.

In what could be interpreted as the politically Conservative Eagleson tweaking an in-power Liberal federal government, the Eagle was to mention as the excitement and tension built across the land before the game: "Hell, they (Ottawa) put $10 million into Canadian Unity, surely they can find a few million for this. What unifies the country more than this? Just go out and talk to people and see what unity is all about when a tournament, and particularly the Russians, are on the way."

In terms of what this represents, the recurring theme through training camp in a sultry hot August had been the eternal one by players involved in such things: if we win, it's expected. If we lose, we're bums.

Galling to the players, though hardly preoccupying as they set out to defend the nation's hockey honor, was the attitude of Ottawa. It wouldn't be until after the game that players who had given their all, including part of their coveted vacation time, to wear their Maple Leaves and assume the risk connected with losing, that they would be able to plan their following day. They had been told, in effect, that win and you'll be given a testimonial dinner in the nation's capitol; lose and you're on your own.

However, and the historical aspects of it will be reviewed in later chapters, this exemplifies the schizophrenia we manifest in hockey. Symbolically, it's the twentieth anniversary of the last Canadian world champion. This was the Trail Smoke Eaters, a band ignored at home, assailed as ruffians in Europe, living below the poverty level during the tournament and going into debt to be there. Their reward? Abuse, a watch and months of deprivation while debts were paid off.

Teams such as this tried to get the message home that the Soviets and Czechs were for real and becoming more real. At home, we chuckled, called them stupid and took unrealistic solace in the feeling we'd turn loose our pros any time there was a lesson to be taught.

The Soviet Union 8, Canada 1.

That was the lesson out of Canada Cup II, a lesson which should have us putting our game under a microscope from the park level through all the rungs of the ladder. One game doesn't a system prove but it does give hints when coupled with two years earlier when the NHL All Stars were walloped in the final of the Challenge Cup. That leaves us with, and unfortunately too many people still cling to it, the near miss win in the first big series in 1972.

The smoke had cleared but the recriminations had not in the days following this setback. Team Canada, not invited to Ottawa, was invited to attend lunch at their hotel with the Prime Minister as guest. Only two players showed up for the meal, another dropped in briefly.

The defeat did galvanize Eagleson to reverse his field on the 'this is my last tournament' conviction. Though he allowed he still wants help from the private sector and/or government, he put it simply: "After all I've put into this, I can't go out a loser."

The pathos of it all was the climate which had players obligated to hide rather than attend lunch. The talk shows in Montreal, and across Canada, sparkled with fury, excuses, condemnations and little by way of rational thought. Even as the team was leaving the ice in the

wake of the game, a fan who had been lustily singing the national anthem and waving his flag before the game, shouted at Bowman: "I wish I had a 16 guage shotgun."

Such is the irony and sadness of it all. Players, coaches and team officials are asked to sacrifice their time and sweat, to display their nationalism and are then pushed into a round room with no corners.

The passage of time will remove the bitterness, unjustified as it may be. Perhaps we'll begin taking a look at England, the nation which invented soccer . . . . the most widely played game in the world . . . and yet has won only one World Cup in its history.

The word doldrums appeared shortly before Canada Cup II plunged into its appointed rounds of the hockey universe.

It came from the Team Canada camp, the camp with which most of us became more intimately involved. Because Canada was the battleground, the other characters in the drama arrived pre-packaged.

The Soviets had formed their attack force deep within Mother Russia, cloaked in the semi-secrecy which is their way but giving rise to speculation this would be the most powerful unit ever. For advance billing, credence was given to that thinking when, a short time before embarking for Canada, the Soviets let it leak that they didn't regard this tournament as one of major importance. This was regarded as the classic Soviet reverse psychology which was interpreted as meaning "because we were embarrassed by a bunch of American college kids in the Lake Placid Olympics eighteen months ago, we regard this as a very important tournament."

Czechoslavakia, with the nucleus of their team defected to Quebec City, furiously rebuilt in the solitude of home while the Finns and Swedes dashed around Scandanavia indicating they could be dark horses but remaining somewhat enigmatic. Team U.S.A. worked hard, and openly, in hockey-rich Minnesota and gave off vibrations of being a worthy contender, bolstered by more pros than ever and the euphoria of that Olympic gold medal. After all, shouldn't a group of highly paid athletes be able to duplicate what smooth cheeked collegians had done?

But the doldrums!

Bob Gainey, the peerless Mr. Everything on the ice and an intelligent, articulate surveyor of the scene off it, used it when he reviewed the team's attitude on tournament eve.

Symbolic of the sacrifice required by teams in the western world, Team Canada was asked — TOLD — to report on the day the Montreal Canadiens were holding their annual golf tournament. That was a stark reminder of summer fun cut short to perform this nationalistic duty-ritual so important to a nation which had given the world hockey but which has been finding it difficult to stay even with, let alone ahead of, practitioners adopting it in such far-flung places as Kiev, Prague, Tampare and Stockholdm . . . not to mention such southern neighbors as Minnesota and Massachussetts.

The doldrums applied to reaction to the long training grind, the monastic life (albeit in the plush Chateau Champlain), the rigid off-ice disciplines imposed by Pierre Page and the harsh on-ice activity dictated by head coach Scotty Bowman. There was the pressure from all quarters, the national pride at stake and the feeling of the classic, eternally present no-win situation. Winning would be expected and natural, losing a disgrace.

It is natural that Canadian players arrived at a point of doldrums. However, outside the training camp in the Montreal Forum, other elements critical to past, present and future Canada Cups swirled. As Gainey was to mention, establishing an important perspective: "People want us to win, expect us to win. We want to win but, let's face it, what makes these international events so in demand is the uncer-

tainty. If any team was a sure winner, things such as this wouldn't have appeal. It's a contradiction that people don't seem to understand. And, let's face it, Canada Cup I was something special because it was just that . . . a first, a novelty. The second time around a lot of new elements come into play and you have to understand them."

Other elements included the tournament being caught in the same spiking inflation affecting everyone and everything else. As chairman Alan Eagleson was to groan: "In 1972, it cost us $13,000 to charter a plane to get the team home. Now it costs that much for a charter between Winnipeg and Edmonton."

Indeed, cost was a battle cry for Canada Cup II and will be a critical factor in the direction this formula will take in the future. Hard-shelled and iron-willed Alan Eagleson won, inherited or simply took over the role of hockey czar in these matters. Love him or hate him, nobody ventures to say he doesn't get things done . . . in this case with a combination of purpose and neck twisting. Lining up the all-important sponsors, putting together television packages, coming to equitable agreements with the outside teams possibly brought him as close to breeding an ulcer as any venture in which he had been previously involved.

But it did come together!

The side effects, however, were severe. The Eagle never has been accused of diplomacy and has been accused, occasionally, with overlooking a key fact. These facets ignited a classic outcry from the public and media when fans began lining up for tickets and discovered that, in order to purchase prime games, they

had to accept a two-for-one package, also buying secondary or less popular games. Blackmail was one of the more polite words applied and, under the savage, unrelenting pressure of media and public, Eagleson yielded. The truce called for refunds for those who had accepted tickets they didn't want and an open, buy what you want, policy the rest of the way.

Tickets — the vital financial lifeline in the delicate life support system of profit or loss in this exercise — also exploded into issues in Quebec City and Winnipeg.

The two cities, miles apart both culturally and geographically, because of the vastness which provides Canada with one of the largest land masses on earth, arrived at similar conclusions for different reasons.

In the east, Québec lawyer Guy Bertrand had long held out for a Team Québec in such exercises. His argument revolved around the fierce nationalism of the province and the fact that so many superstars and plain stars called the French-language their mother tongue. It is unavoidable in any history of Canada Cup II to mention the influence of Bertrand's oratory and demands. The situation existed, exists, and was and is part of the complexity of such matters.

Whie Bertrand may generate sympathy in his own province and even among others in Canada, the situation is far more complex than simply going for a Team Quebec. Should this become a reality, there would be as many points to hammer out as there were for the main tournament. For instance, and hypothetically: a Guy Lafleur is a Quebecois. He is also property of Montreal Canadiens which belongs to Molson, a national as well as an international brewing concern. Would the ownership risk allowing Lafleur to play for a Team Quebec at the risk of offending customers in nine other provinces? That's oversimplification but it outlines the type of points which would be raised.

Bertrand's demands combined with a subdued fury because no member of the Quebec Nordiques was invited to Team Canada's camp, created an icy atmosphere in the ancient and charming capital. When ticket sales began for games there, a pair of them, Quebec City residents stayed away in droves.

Emergency measures were called for and Ottawa answered Eagleson's plea for rescue by accepting the two games. The people of Ottawa, without a pro team in hockey, responded well and another problem was resolved by the skin of its teeth.

Winnipeg does have a professional team and has had one, in two different leagues, for some time now. The people in that city obviously have developed a certain sophistication towards the game and what they want. They found they could easily resist the Soviets vs Czechoslovakia; Sweden vs the Soviets, Sweden-Finland and the Soviets-Finland. They warmed slightly to a dandy game featuring Canada and the Czechs.

Whether Winnipegers felt they were being given meaningless, second-class games or whether they were making their own response to ticket prices and ticket packaging remains open to conjecture. Whatever the reason(s), their indifference was only surpassed by the citizens of Quebec City and the majority of games were played in the sad echoes of nearly empty houses.

Before the tournament reached its mid-way point, after which it would head for the presumably more friendly eastern cities, soul searching had begun. While Winnipeg and Edmonton were seen vital to the tournament in decentralizing it and giving other parts of the country a feeling of involvement, it is hard — regardless of what angers have been ignited by prices or selling techniques — to sell early games, especially those not involving Canada.

Until the gathering begins to acquire shape and form, until the fans

can be certain that the Czechs aren't weak and that the Swedes and Finns are, matches are merely testings of the ice. Resentment can build quickly that cities have been 'used' to establish the tournament and then the mistrusted east — carrying through on one of our more charming national characteristics — gets the crème de la crème.

And within the Perils of Pauline surrounding the birth and growing pains of Canada Cup II, there is need for even more insight to retain the historical perspective.

For starters, Canada Cup II was a year late in delivery. On the four year cycle it should have been in 1980 but Canada's Olympic boycott had the added repercussion of causing the professionals to tread softly in extending an invitation to the U.S.S.R. Many of the professional players voiced strong feelings about it and, on the practical level, who could say whether the Soviets would accept the invitation (even with their love of western currency) or who, in the realm of all-important sponsors, would risk backing it.

Tardiness didn't help. Neither did the fact that only two hockey centres in Canada have the twin assets of being hockey hotbeds and having populations in excess of two million citizens. That one opted out didn't help the cause an iota. Crusty Harold Ballard, who is in the enviable position of being able to make unpopular decisions and effect them, said bluntly and irrevocably that he didn't want the tournament, and especially the Soviets, in his Maple Leaf Gardens.

Stripped of this site, CC II had another thorn driven into its side.

Ballard withstood media attacks which accused him of making a decision for an entire city and for holding that city hostage but the decision remained. A prime market was lost even though other smaller centres were presumed to have benefited . . . and that became a moot point after the turnstile performances in the west where only Ed-

monton, with their Wunderkid Wayne Gretzky on display, showed up with any frequency.

With the tournament swinging east and with the trials and tribulations leading into it compounded by non-turnouts, organizers may have been tempted to turn to Montreal's irrepressible Mayor Jean Drapeau who — during the seemingly insurmountable difficulties leading to the 1976 Olympics — kept his battle cry: "There are no problems . . . only solutions."

With Canada Cup II providing interesting hockey, triggering a certain national emotionalism but also generating problems with monotonous regularity, those at the helm had to start rethinking the question of: where do we go from here?

Perspective is ever important in weighing this game of ours. As the legendary president emeritus of the NHL, Clarence Campbell, never wearied of saying when passions were aroused on defeats abroad, "this is the only game Canada has exported and we should be proud of that. It should be satisfying that other countries have embraced it so fervently that now the students are teaching the teachers."

While logical, it isn't quite the stuff enraged citizenry needs to assuage an ego which has always taken solace in the fact that we are (were) supreme in this one area. The legendary Canadian inferiority complex never had cause to suffer when teams from this country could smother hapless Europeans 30-0 and accept world and Olympic championships practically by default.

As part of their preparation for the tournament, the Soviets were bolstered by the extensive research done by Vladimir Dvorzov and published in Tass. In the giant numbers game so popular in North American sports and now obviously infecting the Soviets, Mr. Dvorzov noted the fact that competition between his country's teams and Canada — ranging from midget through junior and World Hockey Association and all the way up to NHL, embraced

410 games before Canada Cup II. Then he pointed out proudly that the standings stood 282 wins, 96 losses and 32 ties . . . in favor of the U.S.S.R.

It is uncertain whether those numbers influenced Team Canada or not but what they did point out was the serious mental block the ongoing and unchallenged Canadian successes of the past have created. When the Soviets first began coming here to learn, they were scorned as strange men in funny suits and obsessed with taking notes. Even their hockey equipment was ridiculed because the resident experts of the time failed to peek under the attire.

It was in 1957 that a young Halifax lawyer named Gerry Regan, who paid his way through Dalhousie law school by promoting hockey and sportscasting (he succeeded Danny Gallivan as resident sportsman on Halifax radio CJCH) recognized what was happening in the Soviet and went to the world championships in Moscow to begin arranging tours with the U.S.S.R. and Sweden. He watched Canada Cup II as Minister of Labor and Minister of State Responsible for Sport in the federal cabinet.

Six years later, *Weekend Magazine* did an extensive tour of the Soviet and one part of a series was a warning (and a plea) that Canada should begin taking these people seriously. The writer was dismissed as being influenced by environment and/or vodka and the Establishment — both media experts and hockey in general, sat smugly back. Those were the days, with the Soviets catching up to and then passing our amateurs, that the bully cry became the crutch: "If it gets serious, we'll turn our pros loose upon them."

Long, involved, sometimes nasty, often stupid events leading to the first big series in 1972 marked the state of frustration which had been reached. Vital to it was Canada's pullout from all hockey in 1970 when it was supposed to play host to the world championships.

The next shock was '72 and the hairsbreadth win after the same resident experts had predicted an eight game sweep for Canada. Some had even taken the trouble to go to Moscow to 'scout' and came back with the same opinion. They were there but they still couldn't see it.

Lessons have been hard learned but, in the process, the burning desires for both elegant play and pos-sible revenge became epidemic with Canadians.

With the millions of words spoken and written during this year's exercise, some hit the mark with telling accuracy. James Christie penned in the *Globe and Mail:* "Canada's national ego went back into training when the talented recruits of Team Canada 1981 pitched camp in the Montreal Forum . . . ."

"The Canada Cup is a last ditch effort to support a weakening claim to world hockey supremacy. Canada used to be the toughest and strongest kid on the block . . . but the days are long past when senior teams could waltz smugly into world championships. Canada is now just another challenger."

Tough pills to swallow but essential to the cure.

The inventory of achievement and non-achievement during the years when this country should have been responding and countermoving, is sad in that it was real but dismissed. The '72 series was closer than anyone suspected it would be. The WHA tour in 1974 was a 4-1-3 disaster. Augmented by professionals, Canada's visits to world championships are a parade of frustrations: 1977, Vienna, fourth; 1978, Prague, not a bad third; 1979, Challenge Cup (NHL all stars as opposed to Team Canada) shut out in the final.

The background and evolution are essential to understanding what has been happening and possibly in detecting future direction. What has emerged so clearly is that, no matter how many other countries are invited to play, no matter how many more begin taking the game seriously, this remains a struggle between Canada and the U.S.S.R. in the public mind.

This is the only pairing which fuels the full range of passions and which has any meaning.

The chemistry is interesting. On a year to year basis, Czechoslovakia is a legitimate world contender, regardless of the style of competition. The Czechs have their off years, which isn't surprising because their player base is relatively small and they do get raped by defections on occasion. But year in and year out, and many people overlook the fact that hockey is a tradition over there going back to the 1930's when it was a European pioneer, teams from there can stay close to or beat the Soviets and/or Canada.

Yet, the Czechs don't trigger any emotional hungers or angers in Canadians. Perhaps it's because they are identified as the good guys who dislike the Soviets and we can't get angry with them for that. Or perhaps it's simply a matter of style, even though that is a shallow possibility because the playing styles of the Big Three are so similar now.

In the future, the Americans should make the world powers into a Big Four but that isn't likely to arouse too many people, either. They are our neighbors and we are — and will be — exposed to their players nine months a year during regular NHL play. When they become truly and legitimately competitive at this level, they'll generate some enthusiasm but the charisma still belongs to the Soviets.

At the Olympic level, leaders have apoplexy because the gigantic games are often viewed as a showcase for track and field with all other sports merely frills. The same manifestation appears to happen in hockey tournaments: all those other games are staged just to give people something to do until Canada and the U.S.S.R. meet. That curdles organizers who must flog tickets and find sponsors for these 'extraneous' matches but it's difficult to change the public mind about such matters. That's why, by mid-tournament, some editorialists were predicting that tournaments such as this had joined the dinosaur and dodo bird and the only future conflicts with mass appeal would be Canada-U.S.S.R.

Eagleson, ever the eye of a storm but certainly the reigning authority on international hockey, is effusive in his agreement on that point. As the guru in such matters, he is also the man who has the answers to the why, and the how of why — in his opinion —the Canada Cup format won't die. Neither will the hockey future belong to an unbroken chain of exchange trips between Moscow and anywhere in Canada.

Reflecting on the tournament and those who said the formula was finished, Eagleson disagreed. In fact,

he believes it is media misinterpretation of his own stance which may have caused thinking in that direction. As he was to say: "I had said that this was MY last tournament, not that this would be THE last tournament. There's a big difference. I've been at it long enough and I feel it's just too much for one man. The financial responsibility, alone, is too much for one man to assume. But the format itself? The Canada Cup? That's here to stay because it has to be here to stay if we're going to continue with international growth and the international play fans want."

Eagleson doesn't hesitate an iota in acknowledging that — in the exclusive world of hockey — the only matchup everyone wants is Canada-U.S.S.R. He concedes that everyone in both countries wants it but then there is the small matter of the Player's Association, or union, and the intricacies and complexities in putting together the pieces of any international hockey puzzle.

Ruling out any sustained series such as we had in 1972 is the number of players in the NHL who belong to the PA . . . . such as all of them.

Though they don't yet represent a power bloc within the PA, players from the United States, Sweden and Finland are a growing force in the league and within the union. Their numbers swell each year (the day before Canada Cup II ended, 11 new Finns were airlifted to Canada to attend their first pro camps). Though most players won't disguise the fact that such added commitments are an imposition, national pride does flare.

As an example, one tongue-in-cheek Toronto writer editorialized during the tournament that while Bjorn Salming may be injury and illness prone during any given NHL year, he always comes up remarkably healthy when he shrugs into a Swedish national jersey.

What that all means is, if there's going to be major international play in the future, all these transplants want in and wouldn't tolerate Can-

adians and Soviets having exclusivity on nationalism, glamor and the dollars involved.

The dollars are of interest to everyone.

Everyone from the Player's Association (via the pension fund) to the owners, the International Ice Hockey Federation, national associations and Hockey Canada have a deep and abiding mercenary interest in what surplus remains after expenditures. That's another way of saying profit.

From square one, that's why Toronto's refusal to join in the fun was a severe blow in 1981. Because of its population, its licensing and marketing potential, Toronto represented a guesstimate $500,000 in additional revenues. That was missing.

Another blow to income was the late start. The boycott of the 1980 Olympics left many things in limbo for boycotting nations and the tournament was put on the back burner. It wasn't until May 15, 1981, that it really got off the ground. In terms of preparation, selling sponsors, licensees and others, that was five to seven months late if things were to be done properly.

The hue and cry during the months leading to May revolved around the suspicion that the ever enigmatic Eagleson either allows problems to develop or creates them, then comes up the Messiah when he solves them. Whether that's fact or fallacy, the problems did exist and did jeopardize the tournament even further. As late as August 15, television negotiations weren't going as anticipated. The offer was for $1.5 million, organizers felt they couldn't sell for less than $2.1 million. Reflecting on that crisis, Eagleson says candidly: "It was that close . . . . I, we, would have thrown in the sponge right there and then, paid the penalty fee to the IIHF and forgotten the whole thing."

The financial balance is precarious because it must satisfy all parties. The NHL owners consent, albeit grudgingly, to lend players out because the money flowing into the pension fund from the tournament

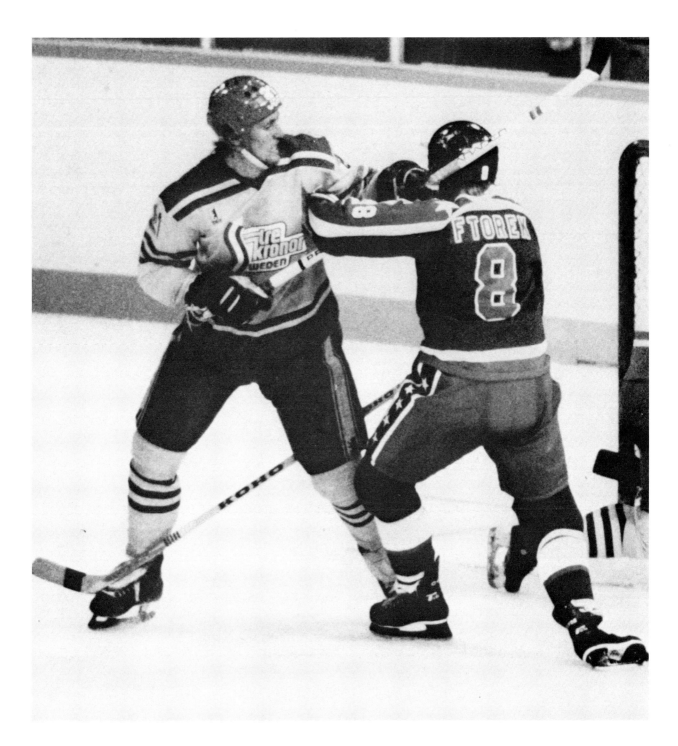

means relief for them in their financial participation. If that relief isn't sufficient, they take long, hard looks at their property. As one general manager mentioned after the injury to Gilbert Perreault "Do you think the Knox Brothers (Buffalo owners) think this is worthwhile, no matter what goes into the pension fund? How do they convince their fans to pay for season seats when a key player will be missing for weeks and weeks?"

The basic numbers for those feasting on the financial pie in 1981 showed $600,000 to the Hockey Canada scholarship fund, $1.4 million to the pension fund and $1.5 million to the IIHF. These are the key figures and there are mutations off them which are important to those involved but which only serve to complicate understanding for anyone else.

As far as the players are concerned, it isn't a magic carpet in immediate financial gain. Participating teams (or their federations) are guaranteed $125,000. In the case of team Canada, the formula worked out was $1,000 for being invited to camp, $1,000 for making the team, $1,000 for finishing second and $2,000 for finishing first (as in winning the final). That comes up to pin money $5,000. There are such side benefits, upon which a price can't be placed, as rings, watches, autographed team photos etc. These have intrinsic personal value in the sense that they are the type of memorabelia which nobody else can have.

Financial participation is essential to all of those sharing in it and, to get what might appear to be a simple project on the road involves an organogram worthy of any corporation. At the base is Hockey Canada and flowing out of it (or, more correctly, into it), the crucial spurs of the IIHF, NHLPA and NHL.

In the middle, but tied by the umbilical cord to the others, is the Canada Cup committee with its satellites: financial, legal, protocol, tickets, TV-radio, licensing and, of course, the teams. Each of these has input, responsibility and vested interest but, in the past, it has always essentially boiled down to what the Eagle calls "The Eagleson Group."

Eagleson doesn't balk at all in his assessment of his group's role in salvaging the 1981 show. Speaking of Hockey Canada and the democracy of committee decisions: "I had found in the past that I'd go to the committee with something, they'd approve it and I'd go back and do what I wanted to do anyway . . . . but at a loss of crucial time. For 1981, the only decision I really took to committee, because the responsibility was so great, involved the decision on Winnipeg (including that, a small market) and the television rights."

In other numbers, estimates comparing 1976 and 1981 were $6.2 million down to $5.5 million gross and an increase in expenses from $3.0 to $4.2 million. It came up a fine balancing act to achieve the financial aims and objectives.

The alternatives are few, even though the financial strain will be greater in the future.

The 'dream' Canada-Soviet rounds have inherent roadblocks. A top team vs a top team (Stanley Cup champion vs European or 'world' champ) faces even larger problems. Identification would be one because NHL clubs now have so many nationalities. And Bill Torrey, GM of the 1980-81 Stanley Cup Islanders, pointed out: "Do you really think my guys would have jumped up and down if, as soon as we had won the Cup, we'd have been committed to playing Russia or whoever next or even in September? I doubt it."

Looking ahead, the tournament format will prevail. If there had been any doubt of that before, it faded when the final result of Canada Cup II was committed to history. A dozen people could come up with a dozen alternatives but each would be shot down for any number of reasons. If there is an alteration in the look of Canada Cup III, it could be in terms of numbers . . . excluding a weak link such as Finland was this year, going to a double round robin to inject more meaning or remaining with a single round robin but with a best of three playoff.

If there was a single festering point following this ambush, it was in the sudden death approach to who got to fondle the enormously heavy nickel Canada Cup. It long has been a sore point with sports purists that one game doesn't prove much excepting that a given team is hot at the right time. The similarity of Canada Cup II and the Lake Placid Olympics makes the case in point. The one difference is that the American collegians were hot, and fortunate, from start to finish and ran into — as one scribe penned — "a Tretiak who couldn't stop a beach ball." In this one, Canada was on a streak from exhibition games through semi-finals but ran into a Tretiak who, on this night, could have blocked darts from a blowgun.

The world didn't end on September 13, 1981. In Canadian context, it merely accelerated our annual autumn depression.

Presumably the name of the game still remains seeing the best hockey on this globe. Most of the time we did. As in any game, and as Bob Gainey had said what semed such a

long time ago, the name of sport is the uncertainty. Even Las Vegas wouldn't be much fun if one knew he or she would be a winner every time.

When someone is invited to a feast, there's no point in ruining it by fretting about calories.

Because we are so intimately involved with it and whether one subscribes to the game being born of soldiers playing a form of shinny or lacross on the ice at Kingston or Halifax, it is easy to lose sight of the exclusivity of the game.

Relative to other sports, such as soccer, and allowing for the amount of the earth's surface which doesn't have winter, only a handfull of countries play the game. Six, or five if you discount a cyclical weak link, are the cream of the crop and most come from different 'systems,' lifestyle and ideologies.

Attempting to make comparisons on any of the above basis is odious. Nor is it significant for those seeking excuses to retreat into the hackneyed idea that the Soviets are a 12 month hockey team. Members of the Soviet national team are just that, members when there IS a national team. Beyond international assignments, they drop back to their own clubs. The amount of preparation time is academic. Some of the more knowledgeable editorialists concluded the training time for Canada, within our lifestyle, was ideal. Longer and everyone would be stale. The Soviets began in July and that suits their lifestyle.

Never-the-less, just as Mike Liut left Team Canada and went to the St. Louis training camp, so did Tretiak report back to his Central Army team where he'll play until next called upon for national service.

And concluding with the exclusive nature of the sport, which more or less lofts it up there with polo, a Canada Cup is more than bragging rights. As much as they keep repeating the world tournament is the real one, the Soviets do know that running through teams from Germany, Italy, Japan or whatever does not represent a valid title. The Canada Cup does. Soviet thinking appreciates that more after a win than a loss but that's only natural.

Meanwhile, in the countdown towards Canada Cup III, Canada will be paying the usual harsh dues which will, in turn, create a torrid demand for the tournament.

Within the intricacies and tradeoffs necessary for presentation of the CC, agreements with the IIHF require Canada to send its token, sacrificial lambs to the world tournament, the Izvestia tournament, junior world championships et al. In these, Canada has no chance of winning and just about any country with any hockey muscle can join in the bragging rights by beating Canada.

With that buildup, a steady flow of angry IOU's, Canada Cup III will be in demand.

3

The Netminders:
The Big Plays,
The Finals,
A Game
By Game Review

Hannu Lassila makes the save.

Ken Dryden watches from the crowd.

Myshkin makes a diving save.

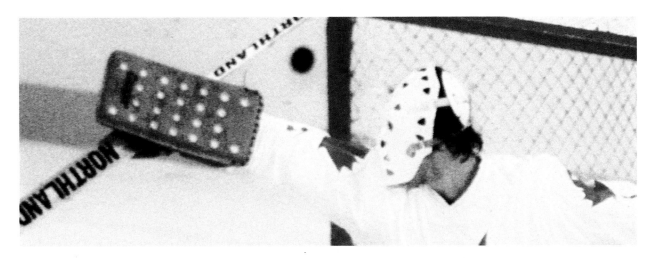

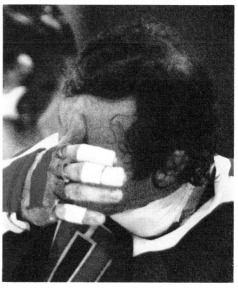

*Russian goalie Vladislav Tretiak
once again proves he's a superstar.*

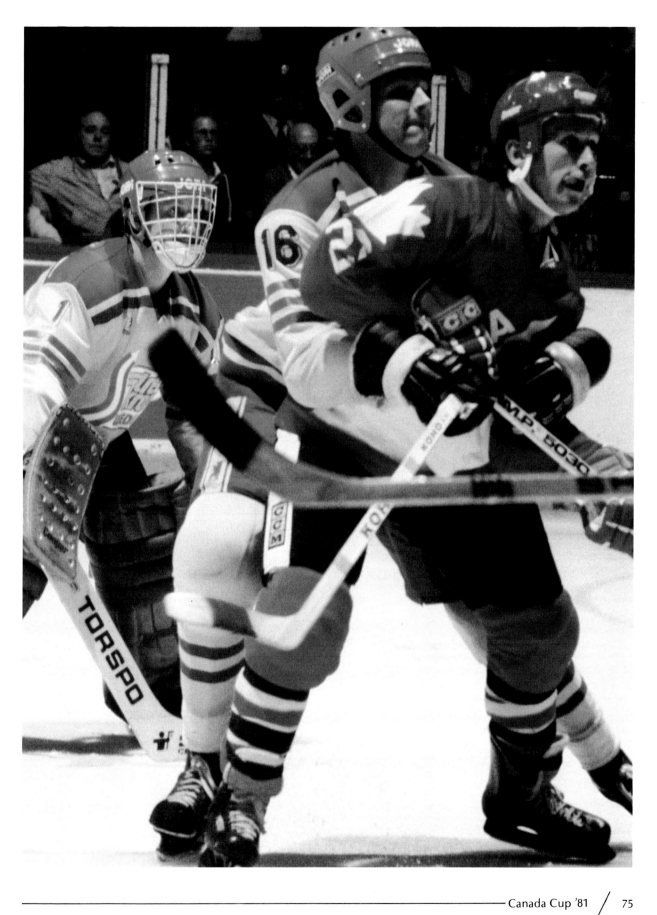

Guy Lafleur is congratulated by Hartsburg and Gretzky.

Team Canada gets strong support in the Edmonton Coliseum.

Gilbert Perreault breaks away.

Gilbert Perreault is lost to Team Canada and The Dream Line is broken up.

Butch Goring is jubilant after scoring.

Anatoly Semyonov.

Wayne Gretzky puts it high to the glove side.   *Rick Middleton scores.*

Guy Lafleur is close.

Guy Lafleur's skating inspired a
popular chant of Guy... Guy...
Guy... in every rink.

Barry Beck is checked by
Alexander Skvortsov.

Marcel Dionne concentrating on
puck.

Vasiliev and Linsman square off.

Miroslav Dvorak

Tretiak!

The Russian team huddles for a strategy conference.

Shalimov moves in for the shot.

Petra Ihnacek puts the boards to good use.

Tretiak and Myshkin — Russia's Dynamic Duo.

Butch Goring about to shoot after beating the defense.

Tony Esposito in goal for Team USA.

*Mike Eaves runs into a tough Team
Canada Defense.*

Wayne Gretzky is beseiged by reporters in the dressing room.

The Face Off.

Tretiak once again makes the save.

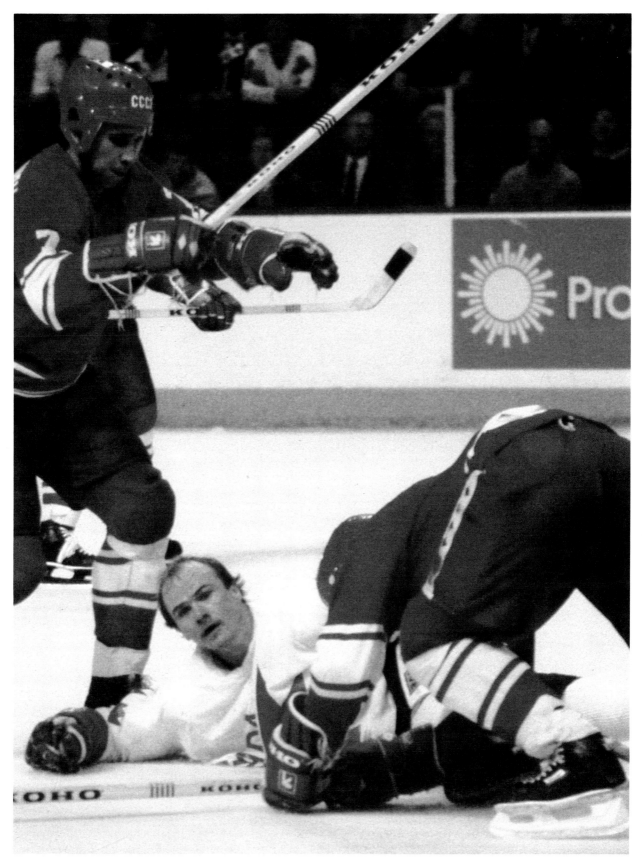

Rick Middleton is knocked to the ice.

Mike Liut watches the first of eight go by him.

Tretiak keeps his eye on the puck.

Sam Pollock.

Canada's well known rose.

Allan Eagleson.

Clark Gillies ties the score at 1-1.

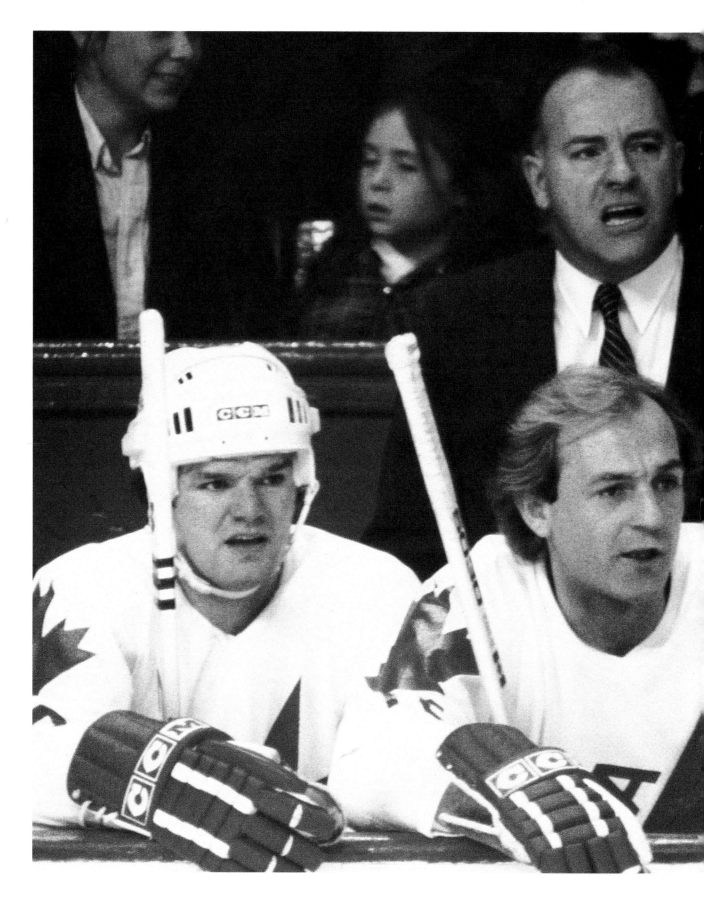

Scotty Bowman's face tells it all.

Tretiak stops a Gretzky shot.

Russia goes ahead.

Concern on the Canadian side of the rink.

Superstar of the series.

Team Canada watches the awards presentations.

Valery Vasiliev and Denis Potvin model hats for photographers.

Allan Eagleson and Pierre Elliot Trudeau present the Canada Cup to Russian captain Valery Vasiliev.

Tretiak and Vasiliev are pleased with their play.

An anticipated three-way deadlock for the top after round one didn't materialize because the Soviets, favored for a win, were forced to struggle for a tie against archrival Czechoslovakia. That allowed the United States and Canada to rule the roost after one day, Canada unleasing the expected fury to crush Finland and the Americans forging a workmanlike win over Sweden.

Canada 9   Finland 0

It had been predicted that the tedium of training camp and the necessary but meaningless exercises of pre-tournament games would bring Canada to its opening match in a frenzied peak, comparable to heavyweight title aspirants who train in monastic privation and arrive finely tuned and savagely ready.

Game but vastly outgunned Finland was the vehicle through which 8,991 fans in Edmonton and millions on national television saw proof that this just might be the finest Canadian team ever assembled.

Gallant and overworked Markus Mattson, sentenced to play in goal for the Finns, managed to hold it to 1-0 for 20 minutes but then the torrent broke and it became 6-0 in the next 20 minutes as all the practice produced a 'team' — well oiled, precise, deadly. A hail of 42 shots was hurled at Mattson while Mike Liut faced few difficult chances in the 24 he handled.

In this dream lineup, it all came to pass on this night. Wayne Gretzky and Guy Lafleur, paired as part of that dream, had six points between them. Gretzky, as did Mike Bossy, had two goals while Lafleur had three assists. The rest of the Canada hit parade listed Ray Bourque, Danny Gare, Bryan Trottier, Butch Goring and Clark Gillies.

The co-feature of opening day was south and east of Edmonton and the oil fields. It was in Winnipeg and even if only 3,516 fans turned out, it was still a crucial one. In a short tournament, any match involving the Soviets — even an opening

— may be considered crucial if the opposition manages to do the unexpected.

Over the past few decades, it has been axiomatic that games between these two sides aren't games as much as political statements. As one journalist penned following it: "Czechoslovakians may not be able to get Soviet troops out of their country but occasionally, on an ice rink, they can stick it to them."

Of the three games on inauguration day, this was the most bitterly, emotionally contested. The Czechs, considered shallow in dept and experience because so many of the nation's stars had jumped to North American dollars, proved they had no deficiencies in heart and spirit.

This was typical of so many matches between the two: nothing pretty, post-game accusations of uncalled fouls . . . just sheer intensity pitching a raw band of proud patriots against what was suspected to be the finest hockey machine yet turned out on the Soviet assembly lines.

It hinted of upset when the Czechs managed to keep it scoreless through the first period and then got a goal from Milan Novy at 1.57 of the second to stun the USSR.

However, stunned or not, the men from the Steppes rarely lose composure and with a million rubles of talent, they hung in, doggedly, until Alexandr Drozdetski equalized eight minutes later.

That was to be it!

Just how determined were the Czechs shows up in the shots on goal: 26-16 in their favor, forcing the brilliant Vladislav Tretiak to call upon all the skills, tricks and cunning a goaltender of his calibre acquires as a repertoire in a decade of top international competition.

At that, and because the Soviets do prefer the 'perfect shot' to the wild numbers game, it remained for Karel Lang to match Tretiak in quality if not in quantity.

United States 3   Sweden 1

Of the five foreign teams in this tournament, Sweden and Team USA personified what is happening in the National Hockey League.

Some editorialists satirized the fact that each of these 'national' sides was, in reality, a talented patchwork quilt of highly paid professionals who had abandoned the jerseys of various cities to come here disguised as nationalists.

Defencemen Rod Langway and Boerje Salming were cases in point, typifying the remainder of their respective lineups. Langway, giving his all for his American birth certificate (actually Taiwan) is normally employed in Montreal. Salming, a Swedish delight as well as a nationalist on these occasions, is using Toronto as home base for stashing away his retirement kronor.

If these teams shared hybrid status, they also shared another quantity: neither loomed a contender to win it all but each packed enough power to (a) finish highly and (b) upset the balance of power with a well aimed upset or two.

Getting them together on opening day, then, represented both an interesting fan attraction and the opportunity for scouts from the 'legitimate' contenders to assess them under battle conditions.

The Americans got some excellent work from new American Tony Esposito (his citizenship arrived just in time for training camp) and the sometimes chippy piece went in favor of the Americans.

Reed Larson and Dave Christian established a 2-0 cushion in the first period and then the American braintrust made what could have been a severe tactical error: it decided to sit on the lead.

This was playing into willing Swedish hands and Thomas Gradin halved the margin in the second period before Team U.S.A. decided to get back to its first period game plan and head off a tactical fatality.

That gave Mike O'Connell the opportunity to get things back on track and the final 3-1 count served as an accurate reflection of play.

Standings after Day One

	P	W	L	T	F	A	Pts
Canada	1	1	0	0	9	0	2
USA	1	1	0	0	3	1	2
Czechoslovakia							
	1	0	0	1	1	1	1
USSR	1	0	0	1	1	1	1
Sweden	1	0	1	0	1	3	0
Finland	1	0	1	0	0	9	0

DAY TWO

Day Two of play was actually day three on the calendar because of the mandatory day in between for rest, regrouping, reflection and travel. The favorites all won but the surprises were Sweden and the United States. Each considered a potential dark horse before the tournament, neither could muster the strength to stay with second round opponents: the Swedes having the score doubled by the Soviets and the Americans falling before an awesome late game explosion by Canada.

Canada 8   United States 3

Head coach Scotty Bowman said after this one: "We learned something out there tonight . . . that we can't afford mistakes. We made mistakes and they cost us."

However, mistakes or not, the much heralded artillery and skill of Team Canada proved itself again. On paper, this was seen a formidable group and on this occasion it proved not to be a paper tiger.

The Americans came to play and did so until a combination of late game collapse and Canada shifting into overdrive detonated a five goal mushroom cloud which buried them 8-3.

If the opening round produced mini-war between ideological opposites Czechoslovakia and the USSR, this joust between the big North American north-south neighbors had a similarity, even though the cultures and ideologies of the two are peas in a pod. For 60 minutes the Good Neighbor policies were abandoned and a certain ferocity intruded.

Even such people as Rod Langway and Larry Robinson, sometimes defence partners and always team-mates during the regular NHL season, met in temper tantrum situations late in the contest.

Before the tournament, head scout for it all, Jim Gregory, had explained the schedule was ideal for Canada in that it was a steady progression towards the power teams. That was based on early handicapping.

He, like others, had felt the Americans were an ideal second opponent because (a) they should be tough but (b) because of familiarity all round, Canada wouldn't lose its poise if trouble appeared.

It turned out to be an accurate assessment all the way.

In effect, it was played out in the manner of a three-act Shakespearian drama for Canada or tragedy for the Americans. Act One was a 1-1 first period in which Canada displayed the same slow starting qualities it had against Finland. However, the slow start was aided by a Team USA which came out with fire and determination, liberal use of the body and the sugar plums of upset dancing in their heads.

Act Two: Canada doing the expected by establishing a 3-1 lead after two periods but with no hint of the Americans surrendering.

Act Three: a shocking twist of plot for 11,348 fans in the Northlands Arena and astonished television viewers from coast to coast. Neither side had been able to capitalize on a total of 17 power play opportunities but then Dean Talafous broke the string and less than a minute later Mark Johnson flashed one behind Mike Liut and it was a tie game.

Were the Americans living up to their dark horse, spoiler potential?

It was a brief flirting with such matters because what had seemed to be a sleeping giant suddenly became aroused. Team Canada poured in five goals in approximately 10 minutes and that was that.

Tony Esposito, the wise Tony O, couldn't keep up with the torrent.

Seen as the main cog in defensive plans, Tony wasn't as sharp as he might have been during the flood of goals. However, when the raw scoring power snapped into gear, few goalers in the world could have prevented the outcome. The differ-

ence between a sharp Esposito and a less than sharp goaler at this stage would have been merely the difference in the margin.

In the final statistics, Canada had outshot the Americans 36-31, a proximity of figures which also was noted by Bowman who thinks in terms of low shots against.

Once again, the sheer elegance of the Gilbert Perrault, Wayne Gretzky, Guy Lafleur line rewarded the price of admission. They piled up a total of nine points, Gretzky getting two goals, two assists, Perreault two goals, one assist and Lafleur two helpings.

Bryan Trottier was a two goal man and others went to Marcel Dionne and Mike Bossy. Steve Christoff had opened the scoring for Team USA.

Czechoslovakia 7   Finland 1

Any ideas lingering to the effect that Finland may have had an off game against Canada were dispelled when Czechoslovakia came out and mauled them just as thoroughly.

It was the first opportunity to weigh another team against Canada on the basis of a mutual opponent and, even though still early in the tournament, second, revised looks were being taken at the Czechs. Any suspicion that defections such as the Stastnys had removed their heart was fading. Somewhere, in their limited but obviously quality reservoir of playing talent, a Christian Bernard was available and busy doing the transplants to keep the heart healthy.

Put on the shelf for the moment, as well, was thinking that the opening 1-1 result against the Soviets was the product of playing over their heads on political grounds.

The job against Finland was accomplished with elan, with spirit and in the face of mounting woodchopping as the Finns became understandably frustrated.

At this stage of the tournament, were a medal to be struck for basic heroics above and beyond the call of duty, it would have gone to goaler Hannu Lassila who braved 53 shots and gave the appearance, to the final whistle, that he felt his team could come back if only he did his job.

In contrast, Czechoslovakia cloned its defence: allowing the same number of shots (16) as in the Soviet game.

The only semblance of competition came in the first period when Lassila's work kept it to 2-1. After that, it was Gone With The Wind . . . the wind being Czech skaters who foraged around the Finn goal with the instincts of lemmings going to the sea.

Another tipoff to what this youthful group of Czechs was all about appeared in the scoring parade . . . because it was that, a parade. The scattergun threat indicated the same balance as the USSR and, by the end of this one, anticipation was building by leaps and bounds for the upcoming Day Three schedule which would feature Canada and Czechoslovakia in what no longer remained a throw-in schedule-filler.

Jiri Lala produced two goals for the winners and the rest were distributed among Pavel Richter, Miloslav Horava, Norbert Kral, Arnold Kadlec and Darius Rusnak.

Reliable Matti Hagman was the lone marksman for Finland which tried to shake up the troops for this one by pulling veteran defenceman Timo Nummelin from the lineup. It didn't work!

Soviets 6   Sweden 3

Anyone attempting to research the Soviet-Sweden match might be fooled by the score. The final 6-3 doesn't appear overly formidable and the fact it stood at 3-2 after two periods might lead one to believe it was a gangbuster until it broke open.

Closer analysis would disclose several things, the least praiseworthy being that the Swedes brought in a chippiness which did little to thrill the scant (3,200) crowd which showed up.

Most of the Swedes in this lineup toil for NHL teams and the majority noted for playing skills, docile behavior and disclinination to indulge in physical presence. Against the Soviets, the wraps were off and resident experts were a trifle less than amused.

After all, the Soviets are always under orders to play hockey and back off — painful as it may be, at

time — from disorderly conduct generated in their direction. The Swedes, apparently responding to this knowledge, spent much of the game chopping people who couldn't chop back and then complaining they were victimized by officiating.

The Soviets, for their part, were taciturn in accepting the bumps and bruises but were delighted with the windfall profits.

The windfall was especially appreciated because the Soviet power play had gone pfft in their game against Czechoslovakia and this represented a restoration of confidence.

That confidence was supported by four power play goals and, to really rub it in, a shorthanded effort. Five of six goals on either extra man or shorthanded situations had to serve to put the USSR back into a groove they may have been knocked from in their opener. They also came away with the confidence of knowing they had survived, and rather well, what everyone fears in a short tournament: a hot goaler. Pelle Lindbergh played as well as anyone could play but it wasn't enough.

The power play served as the sledgehammer which put the Swedes behind a 2-0 eight ball in the first period. Sergei Kapustin scored one of his two goals for the evening and then Sergei Makarov struck. After that, Sweden had its fits and starts between slashes and chops and Lindbergh managed to keep it to 3-2 after 40 minutes. Then the wheels came off for Sweden.

Alexandr Maltsev, Alexei Kasatonov and Vladimir Krutov rounded out the winning scoresheet. Anders Haakansson, Anders Hedberg and Lars Molin were the scorers of record for Sweden.

Standings after Day Two

	P	W	L	T	F	A	Pts
Canada	2	2	0	0	17	3	4
Czechoslovakia	2	1	0	1	8	2	3
USSR	2	1	0	1	7	4	3
USA	2	1	1	0	6	9	2
Sweden	2	0	2	0	4	9	0
Finland	2	0	2	0	1	16	0

DAY THREE

Day Three brought several points into clear perspective. One, in what was considered the primary game of the day, Czechoslovakia proved that it wasn't listening to the handicappers and was armed with the confidence to stay in the title hunt until the end. And, two, the Americans received all but the coup de grace as the adrenalin of Lake Placid was finally replaced by reality at the hands of the Soviets. In the all-Scandinavian joust, Sweden gained some measure of dignity while Finland proved it was overmatched in this group of teams.

Canada 4   Czechoslovakia 4

If it was any consolation, the Big Game in Winnipeg once again proved Scotty Bowman a soothsayer. He had been saying all along that Czechoslovakia wasn't a dark horse and everyone should revise their thinking or they'd run into trouble at the hands of the pesky and determined 'rebuilding' team. The 4-4 result against Canada proved him correct.

His other crystal ball venture went all the way back to the previous June when he gambled on a youngster named Jiri Dudacek in the National Hockey League's entry draft. Bowman had rated Dudacek the pick of the European litter and gambled that, with the idea planted in his head, the player now regarded as the best junior in the world would be tempted to join the east to west Atlantic airlift and join Bowman's Buffalo Sabres.

Dudacek's play in this crucial game — and all games are crucial in a short tournament — proved Bowman right again even if it caused a stinging result in tournament play. However, the ever realistic Bowman said following the match that the result was appropriate in terms of the night's play.

For the Czechs, this was a case of all's well that ends well because they got off on the wrong skate when

their opening lineup was caught with a mistake in it and they were in a shorthanded situation off the top with a minor penalty.

They weathered that storm and proceeded to stun 10,392 fans in the stadium while bolting television viewers to their chairs across the land by hammering in two goals for a 2-0 lead.

Saturday Night hockey is a tradition in Canada and this match was to revive the good times and memories which made it what it is today. Eager, proud, with little to lose, the Czechs skated and fought, stood up to the best Canada could muster, neutralized Gilbert Perreault, Wayne Gretzky and Guy Lafleur,

and had people across the land wondering just which experts had misguided them into thinking this team was an underdog.

In terms of the opening period, Canada found itself working uphill for the first time in the tournament and showed heart of its own in digging into resources of charcter and pride. With its big line shut down, Team Canada was to get half its production from gentlemen normally defined as top quality utility men rather than glamorous superstars.

For instance, all-rounder Bob Gainey had given Canada a brief but welcome 4-3 lead in the third period and Butch Goring had kept

things alive earlier with a shorthanded goal. That left two goals for the glamor people and they came from Marcel Dionne.

Dudacek?

He opened and closed it!

Less than six minutes into the game he gave Czechoslovakia a 1-0 lead and, at 15:21 of the last period, he wiped out Gainey's goal and created the final result. Around him, other goals came from Jindrich Kokrment and Norbert Kral.

In the see-sawing of this one, it was 2-0 Czechs and 2-2 by the end of the period. Then it went 3-2 Canada, 3-3, 4-3 Canada and then Dudacek.

On the night's play, there was as little to choose as the score would indicate. Canada outshot the Europeans 33-29 and Karel Lang probably had more difficult chances than Mike Liut, but it was, as Bowman said, a legitimate result.

Within the Canadian camp, one roster change was forced by the day of the game practice. Billy Smith, a vocally reluctant backup man to Liut, got his wish — the hard way — to head back to Long Island to enjoy a vacation before his Islanders opened camp. He suffered a broken finger in practice and that meant an emergency airlift of Don Edwards.

Under tournament rules, teams kept two goalers but an emergency reserve was allowed on the roster even though he couldn't remain on site even to practice. Fortunately, and even with the air controllers' situation as it was in the United States, connections between Buffalo and Winnipeg were healthy and Edwards was in time for the game.

Sweden 5   Finland 0

Winnipegers were offered a double-header but managed to all but ignore the leadoff game between Sweden and Finland. In the opinion of people who assess such matters, respect for the wisdom of that city's people rose considerably in the wake of their collective decision to attend to Saturday afternoon shopping instead of going to the rink.

This game, for the unofficial Scandinavian Championship of the Canada Cup, proved to be the first real yawner of the week.

With Denmark and Norway missing, the Swedes were able to lay claim to that unofficial Nordic crown but — and unless — they lost touch with reality they came away knowing it was a shallow victory.

In three games, Finland had managed precisely one goal and the only player of note emerging was Hannu Lassila. In a combination of skill and survival instinct, the goaler had established himself as the only Finn to catch the crowd's fancy and to appear on a level in keeping with the tournament.

Lassila kept the score to 1-0 for 40 minutes but the combination of exhaustion, waves of Swedes and even further breakdowns among his skaters cracked it open in the third period.

Proponents of the European style game, with its sheer skating and absence of hitting, loved this one. However, the majority of those sitting in, either forcibly or voluntarily, came away convinced there is something to be said for the type of hitting manifested on this continent.

How bad were the Finns? Bad enough that when the Swedes were going through a brief period of hacking and chopping (as one editorialist penned: "They did this until discovering the Finns would retaliate") they were offered a two man advantage for 58 seconds. In almost a minute of playing five against three, they didn't manage a shot at Lindmark.

In all, Sweden held a 32-28 shooting edge which hardly reflected either the play or the quality of shots. Expatriate Swedes who now call either Rangers or Islanders home scored four of the five goals.

Anders Kallur struck twice and Anders Hedberg and Ulf Nilsson once each to cause celebrations on Broadway and in the wilds of Long Island. The other went to Bengt Lundholm.

Soviets 4   USA 1

The Soviet Union remained in the ranks of the unbeaten and remained tied with Canada for the top via a patient, workmanlike 4-1 win against a United States team which was presumed to be psyched up by memories of the Olympic medal the previous winter.

However, pros find it difficult to get as charged up about these things as do collegians and the intensity wavered. On the other hand, this was the first chance for revenge for the Soviets and even though they disclaimed any ideas of that being a factor, the result was satisfying to them. Before and after the match the USSR spokesmen dismissed 'revenge' on the basis that "all matches are important to us."

As they did against Canada, the Americans did stay in the game for a long time. With a defence oriented squad, they managed to win the battles along the boards and in the corners most of the way but ran into fatal circumstances when lured into a skating game, for which they weren't equipped.

In the sequel to the game, Team USA management concluded that the lack of a true sniper remained the difference between this club and the major powers. General manager Lou Nanne explained later that "this (legitimate scorers in the 50 goal bracket) still isn't being produced in the US and that has to be our next step."

The lack of fire power, combined with the usual brilliance of Vladislav Tretiak, was glaringly apparent during the first 40 minutes when the Americans fired 20 shots his way but could cash in only once.

As usual, the Soviets played their skating, patient style and went for the 'perfect' shot. At that, they had their highest output to this point (29) and it remained for Tony Esposito to keep it respectable.

Igor Larionov pushed the USSR into a 1-0 lead and the Americans had a flicker of hope when Neal Brotan tied it in the second. However, Victor Zhlutov broke the tie with what proved to be the game winner and Vladimir Krutov made it 3-1 by the end of the second. Vladimir Golikov's third period goal was simply icing on the cake and the final nail in the Lake Placid revenge coffin. The game did have appeal, though, and attracted 13,482 fans to the Edmonton rink.

Standings After Day Three

	P	W	L	T	F	A	Pts
Canada	3	2	0	1	21	7	5
USSR	3	2	0	1	11	5	5
Czechoslovakia							
	3	1	0	2	12	6	4
USA	3	1	2	0	7	13	2
Sweden	3	1	2	0	9	9	2
Finland	3	0	3	0	1	21	0

DAY FOUR

Day Four was one of shocks and shattered dreams and two thirds of the tournament moved east where the character of the piece altered slightly. Canada's nip and tucker against Sweden created worried frowns, the Americans stunned the upstart Czechs to all but mathematically clinch a semi-finals berth while

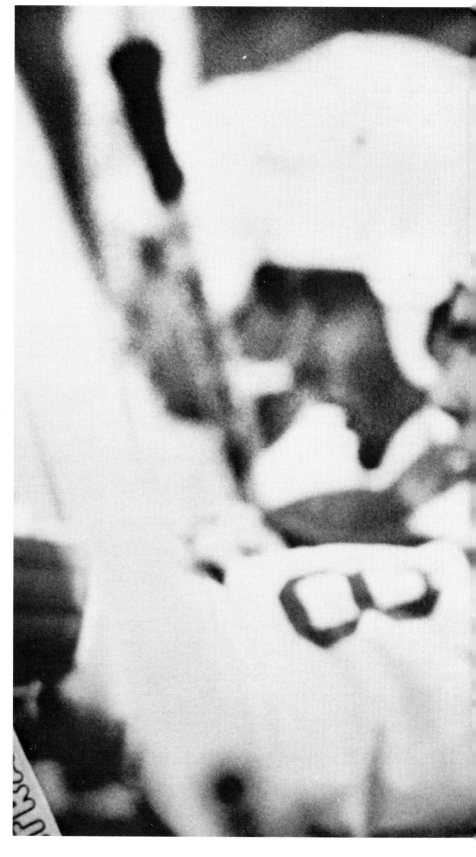

the Soviets allowed Finland their closest match of the tournament to begin what amounted to part two of the round robin.

Canada 4   Sweden 3

From comparative earlier performances by the two teams, Canada was supposed to trample Sweden when play shifted to 'home base' in the Montreal Forum for Labor Day. The Swedes, ever full of surprises, found spirit which had been missing and took advantage of a Canadian team which was obviously looking ahead 48 hours to a big date with the USSR.

Aside from the shock of being forced to fight for a one goal win, Canada suffered a huge loss when Gilbert Perreault suffered a broken ankle in the third period, shortly after his third goal in four games had insured the win.

Most of the post-mortems surrounded what the gilt-edged line of Perreault, Wayne Gretzky and Guy Lafleur had meant to the team through the tournament to that stage. Allowing for the fact they had been shut down in one game completely, their total of 25 points (eight of the goals) came up all the more remarkable.

With the Dream Machine broken up by the injury, the coaching staff looked forward to the off day to discover just what cog could be used as a replacement.

There was also tournament disappointment in the fact only 11,603 fans turned out and whether this was because of the long weekend, the fact the Swedes didn't appear to be much of an opponent or a boycott of ticket prices remained the question.

The game started according to form, with Canada bouncing 2-0 in the first period. The danger signals began to be recognized when, after 40 minutes, it was still only a two goal lead, 3-1. Even at that, Sweden had been inclined to surrender late in such matches but this time they didn't and it went to the wire. Lind-

mark had a great game in goal and Mike Liut only a so-so effort in a 33-16 shooting gallery.

Behind Perreault, Denis Potvin, Mike Bossy and Lafleur were the scorers. For Bossy, it was his fifth in four games. Anders Hedberg put away two for Sweden and Anders Kallur the other.

United States 6   Czechoslovakia 2

The Canada game wasn't the only stunner at the Forum. Later, on the same day, the Czechs strode confidently into the shrine to take on what loomed as comparatively easy pickings in an American side which lacked sound offensive punch and which still hadn't come together.

When it had cleared, the Czechs must have wondered if this was Lake Placid revisited. Even though they were missing the injured Pavel Richter and Radislav Svobodo, the Czechs might have expected a difficult time of it . . . but certainly not a loss of this magnitude, or any magnitude.

Just as shocking as the result, and certainly important to it, was the breakdown of spunky goaler Karel Lang who had been a mainspring in earlier successes. When the American avalanche began in the third period, Lang was lifted and Jiri Kralik was sent in to stem the tide.

Karlik managed fairly well for a cold goaler but the game was out of reach and the two he allowed simply made the score one-sided as opposed to impressive. Proving professionals can stand up with the collegians (such as those who won at Placid), an emotional Dean Talafous said later: "This is the proudest moment of my life."

Talafous, along with Mike Eaves, hammered in two for the unpredictable Americans while Richie Dunn and Warren Miller hit for the others. Jindrich Kokrment provided the losers with a 1-0 first period lead and Darius Rusnak made it 2-0 as the Czechs at least started according to form. Then the wheels fell off.

USSR 6   Finland 1

Once again Winnipegers managed to avoid the rink (2,142 showed up) and those who stayed away missed out on Finland's most noble effort to date. They stayed within five goals of the Soviets and also celebrated scoring their second in four games . . . a certain nobility of achievement when stacked against their first three games.

However, like an immovable object, the USSR wasn't overly moved by the surprising resistance which allowed them only a 2-0 first period lead and a 3-1 two period margin after it had been briefly, and shockingly, 2-1.

Obviously the Soviets felt comfortable and weren't pressing it when Vladimir Krutov, Nikolai Drozdetski and Sergei Makarov had built a 3-1 wall around Ilkka Sinsalo's goal. Possibly as Canada was suspected of doing in another city and another time zone, the Soviets were looking ahead and saving energy for the big head to head with Canada.

They did a workmanlike job and salted it away in a flourish of power play and shorthanded goals. Victor Shalimov and Vyacheslav Fetisov fired power play markers behind Mattson and Victor Zhluktov made the only effort at rubbing it into the hapless Finns when he scored while his team was two men short.

The strange statistic reflected just how much skating room the Soviets allowed. That was in the final 31-24 (for USSR) shots on goal total.

Standings After Day Four

	P	W	L	T	F	A	Pts
Canada	4	3	0	1	25	10	7
USSR	4	3	0	1	17	6	7
USA	4	2	2	0	13	15	4
Czechoslovakia							
	4	1	1	2	14	12	4
Sweden	4	1	3	0	12	13	2
Finland	4	0	4	0	2	27	0

DAY FIVE

The end of the round robin came mercifully for Sweden and with a dollop of consolation for Finland before that team headed home. The Finns managed a 4-4 result with the United States and so went home with one point. The Swedes ran into a Czech team which was fresh off the stinging loss to the Americans and obviously fired up. Canada ? THE game of the tournament for most fans turned into a rout to the delight and surprise of Forum and television fans.

This created semi-finals with friendly neighbors Canada and the United States and the ideological opponents Czechoslovakia and the Soviets.

Canada 7   Soviets 3

Coaches Bowman and Tikhonov had surprises when the game around which most people felt the tournament revolved was played in the Montreal Forum. When a refreshing (compared to other turnstile counts) 16,001 fans settled into their seats, Vladimir Myshkin was in goal for the Soviets and Don Edwards for Canada.

The Soviets explained that "there is no No. 1 goaler in our system . . . everyone is equal" while Bowman said Edwards needed work so he'd have game conditions under his belt for the playoff games. For those who remember the pistol hot Roggie Vachon working the entire 1976 Canada Cup, this came as a startling move, even though Bowman had been hinting at it for days. The switch from Tretiak was more shocking and speculation was that Tikhonov hoped the bouncy little man would duplicate his feat which saw him shut out Team NHL in the Challenge Cup.

Omens, portents, gambles or whatever weren't to help because, after being held to 2-2 for 40 minutes, Canadian firepower kicked into overdrive once again and five goals

were blown past Myshkin in another display of raw, unharnessed scoring power.

The Canadian shift in goal was voluntary but Bowman's other major move wasn't. The decision on who would replace the injured Gilbert Perreault involved Marcel Dionne. It had come down to either Dionne (because of the similarity of skating style and experience) or the more robust Rick Middleton. The group decision favored slickness over added muscle and Dionne replied with his best game and the line flew.

The trio combined for eight points, each getting a goal, Gretzky and Dionne adding two assist and Lafleur one.

As had been the situation in several previous games, Canada required time to get going. Gretzky supplied a 1-0 first period lead and Lafleur made it 2-0 before Igor Larionov and Sergei Shepelev knotted it in the second.

That made the third period the time of decision and it was no contest. Middleton, Dionne, Denis Potvin, Mike Bossy and the redoubtable Butch Goring (assisted by his alter ego Bob Gainey) salted it away. That made Sergei Makarov's game closing goal a token to prove the losers weren't quitters.

Canada held a 33-23 shooting edge on the night and Edwards, though needing a few big saves, indicated that he was ready after the long summer's layoff and then being relegated to Buffalo as the odd goaler out until Billy Smith was injured.

Finland 4   USA 4

The tragi-comedy of Finland was manifested in the earlier game at the Forum on this windup day of round robin play.

After all the indignities the Finns had suffered at the hands of their tournament fellows, they lined up at the blueline for their national anthem before this joust and soon dissolved into puzzlement and bewilderment before shrugging, break-

ing ranks and skating around for the remainder of the music.

The final indignity?

Somehow, whoever was in charge of the turntable at the Forum put on the record of the Italian anthem. Pleasant as it may be, it wasn't the Finnish and there was some speculation that this was enough to rouse them for the tie.

The pathos continued after the match. In what should have been a reasonably happy dressing room, coach Valevi Numminen was to offer the most heart rending quote of the tournament: "I hope the big hockey countries weren't offended by us," he said sadly.

It would be hard for anyone to have been offended by the Finns who came over as a necessary miscalculation if it was to be a six team meet. There aren't any options and organizers had their fingers crossed that they might play over their heads, just as a bridge master mutters prayers of hope when paired with an unknown quantity in a big match.

If nothing else, the Finns left on a note which they hadn't achieved through four games: they left 9,412 fans entertained!

To most, a tie is like kissing your sister but the Finns, managing to do everything the hard way this year, did it with a flair.

They hadn't gained a point, they had scored a total of two goals and they were facing an American team which had upset the Czechs to throw out hints it might be ready for a surprise or two.

The surprise was there but it took awhile to generate.

After a 1-1 first period, the Americans gathered steam and the play appeared to be on its way to predictability when the US moved ahead 3-2 in the second and then 4-2 early in the third. It then remained for Markku Kiimalainen and Arto Javanainen to slam goals before first-time starter Steve Baker to forge the draw and mini upset. Earlier goals had come from Risto Siltanen and Jukka Porvari.

Neal Broten beat Lassila twice for the US and Tom Gorence and Warren Miller once each.

As in the Canada-Soviet game, the Americans had their goaltending surprise as they opted to rest veteran Tony Esposito for the playoffs ahead while exposing Baker to tournament pressure. Baker wasn't entirely enchanted with the experience: "The way we were playing we should have had 10 goals," he growled. With a 46-22 shooting margin, he was probably right. Then again, the critics were to mention he allowed two suspect goals so it evened out.

At least the Finns didn't complain.

Czechoslovakia 7   Sweden 1

It used to be axiomatic around the National Hockey League that one went out of one's way to avoid angering Frank Mahovlich. The big M cruised around doing his thing until riled up and then he did his thing in superstar style.

The Czechs had been the darlings of the upset class through three games of the tournament and they didn't take kindly to being upset themselves by the USA. It was natural that they'd come out on all cylinders against their next opponent, the unfortunate Swedes.

Only 2,988 Ottawa fans sat in on this one but they saw Czechoslovakia at its best as the score built to 2-0 in one period and 5-1 in two. If the Swedes had shown inconsistency in other games, they were given little opportunity to show anything in this one.

Darius Rusnak and Jiri Dudacek were the main tormentors with two goals apiece while the other three were divided among Jaroslav Pouzar, Jiri Lala and Miloslav Horava. Karel Lang lost his shutout bid to Lars Molin.

The onslaught didn't look too impressive in the shooting statistics (33-29 for Czechoslovakia) but the pain of it all was too much for starting goaler Peter Lindmark.

When the count reached 4-0 he skated to the bench and signalled Pelle Lindbergh that it was his turn to be in the wrong end of the shooting gallery.

Standings After Round Robin

	P	W	L	T	F	A	Pts
Canada	5	4	0	1	32	13	9
USSR	5	3	1	1	20	13	7
Czechoslovakia	5	2	1	2	21	13	6
USA	5	2	2	1	17	19	5
Sweden	5	1	4	0	13	20	2
Finland	5	0	4	1	6	31	1

Scoring Power

Leaving the round robin behind and getting into the serious business of sudden death playoff, fans — and team organizers — had time to reflect upon a Team Canada which finished first and did, indeed, exhibit the fire power expected of it.

In opting for dazzling skaters and great scorers, organizers had put together a side which was able to work its way out of any tight corner on sheer scoring power. The 'final' round robin statistics showed a shock squad of five at the head of the scoring list before an outside name appeared.

Number One was Gretzky with five goals and six assist for 11 points. Then it was Lafleur 2-8-10, Perreault 3-6-9, Mike Bossy 6-2-8 and Bryan Trottier 1-7-8.

Where these attack figures became significant was in the comparative analysis of who did what by team on offence and defence. While Team Canada had allowed the same number of goals (13) as both the Soviets and Czechs, it scored 12 more than the second place USSR and 11 more than Czechoslovakia.

In a comparison with 1976, Canada outscored the opposition 22-6 while finishing first with one loss. Roggie Vachon's brilliant average of just over a goal a game showed the different emphasis between the two units. In fact, in '76, the highest scoring team was the USSR with 23 but they had allowed 14.

DAY SIX SEMI-FINALS

The semi-finals pairings came up with no surprises, only duplicate scores and the outcome of providing the hockey masses with what they felt this was all about: A Canada-Soviet Union final.

Played in Ottawa and Montreal, the semi-final games may have followed form but their execution on the ice differed drastically. The Soviets regrouped from their loss to Canada and came out a precision machine against the Czechs. Canada built an early lead against the United States and then, inexplicably, reverted from super to ordinary.

Soviets 4   Czechoslovakia 1

The unemotional facade of the Soviets cracked during the gap between the team's loss and its semi-final game. At least it failed to stand up for coach Victor Tikhonov who fell into the western coaching pit of actually shouting. There wasn't a full-fledged tantrum of shouting match but Tikhonov did actually raise his voice and look angry at practice . . . a most unSoviet thing to do.

The shock value must have been stunning because his team came out working as smoothly and inexorably as a fine Swiss watch (or, as they'd prefer, a Lada) and meticulously picked apart a Czechoslovakian team which finally had its youth and vulnerability exposed by veterans going with metronomic predictability.

In classic understatement, losing coach Ludek Bukac was to sigh following the hockey lesson: "We started badly in the first period . . . I don't know why."

The 'rested' Tretiak was back in goal and played with brilliance which wasn't needed until the Czechs recovered from their initial shock and came back in commendable style to salvage honor if not goals.

In yet another historical footnote out of the series, for the first time in one of these major confrontations involving professionals and European 'amateurs,' a penalty shot was called and successful.

That resulted in the USSR's fourth goal and Sergei Shepelev's second of the game. It was created when Arnold Kadlec fell on the puck in the goal crease and American referee Bob Henry unhesitatingly gave the free shot signal. Shepelev used a tidy little shift and fake to get around the brilliant young Karel Lang to score.

The experts called this display by the Soviets close to perfection and it was all of that as they raced into their big lead. Along with Shepelev, Vladimir Golikov and Victor Shalimov also scored. For the Czechs, breaking the shutout was about the only goal they could hope to achieve in this game and that was accomplished by Jiri Lala in the third period.

While the Soviets were perfection, the Czechs at least showed they had heart . . . even though that part of their arsenal never has been in dispute. After being outshot 13-4 in the opening period, they surged back for a 13-5 margin (27-24 in the match) in the second.

However, with the Soviets following their game plan and textbook religiously, most Czechoslovakian shots were from long distance or while off balance with a defender hanging on. The intensity of the game, as it had been in their 1-1 tiff during the round robin, generated the same edgy level of anger which usually features meetings between the two and it finished threatening the first outbreak of violence in the tournament.

Canada 4   United States 1

The result of the other semi-final was known by the time the Canadians and Americans skated onto Forum ice before 15,000 fans. If the air wasn't quite electric (they were saving that for the final) it was at least edging on playoff level and everyone settled down for a 'meaningful' game.

The incentive had the added dimension of confidence that the arch-rival Soviets had secured their place in the finals with their game in Ottawa, 120 miles west.

Canada came out with the necessary vim and vigor and for 20 minutes had the place oohing and aahing with the precision and complete domination of an American side which was relegated to running in circles trying to catch up with the fleet opposition and the intricate, always in motion and always pressing forward, passing.

The American cause wasn't helped at all when the veteran Tony Esposito came up with a case of early game jitters and allowed long, soft goals by Brian Engblom, and Mike Bossy. Those goals made it 2-0 before the Americans could even begin thinking of how to solve Team Canada's attack so it became — and happily for Canada — a case of Team USA fighting uphill from the eight minute mark.

Bossy fired his second of the game and eighth of the tournament to make it a snug and smug 3-0 after the first period and, perhaps, it was too smug and snug because Canada came out in the second playing as though nobody in a red jersey had ever met anyone in a similar shirt before.

Experts throughout the building and televisionland were muttering dire thoughts that the Canadians were making the mistake of feeling secure about this game and had their minds 24 hours in the future. The more severe analyzed that Canada had, indeed, started the game in that frame of mind and was fortunate to catch Esposito jittery for awhile.

Regardless, after mauling the Americans 3-0 on a 10-2 shootout in 20 minutes, Canada was somewhere in wonderland the rest of the evening and emerged fortunate that the Americans had the same deficiencies they showed through other games, the most notable being a sustained attack and a top quality shooter.

Mike Eaves averted the shutout when he beat Mike Liut in the second but Marcel Dionne regained the three goal cushion when he scored in the third — a period during which Canada did, at times, show a semblance of putting it back together.

On the night, Team USA was outshot 23-17.

In reviews of the day's play, the two big questions appeared and would nag everyone until the showdown to come on Sunday night.

(1) — Had the Soviets been playing possum earlier, especially in their tie with the Czechs and

(2) — Was Team Canada beginning to show wear and tear or was it simply a case of looking a game ahead and forgetting the one at hand.

DAY SEVEN
THE CHAMPIONSHIP

Fears that Team Canada had gone stale in their semi-final match against Team USA were allayed briefly in a torrid first period which saw Vladislav Tretiak the difference between a scoreless situation and the beginnings of a rout. However, the joy was short lived as the Soviets steamrollered back to stun the live audience into silence by smothering TC in a shocking avalance of goals.

Soviets 8   Canada 1

The electricity fairly crackled in the Forum as 17,033 fans — among them the Prime Minister, the Governor General and assorted other VIP's — took their seats to watch what was supposed to be a mop up operation, a coup de grâce, by Team Canada.

As in all such encounters, this was well beyond 'just a game' or bragging rights in hockey. It was a happening, it was on home ground and it revived the memories of past frustrations and humiliations at the hands of these men from the Steppes. After all, this was our game, our turf and hadn't Canada raced through (with the exception of a tie and a stuttering win over the USA) the exhibition round, round-robin and semi-final in fine style. Hadn't one enthusiastic journalist christened them "Team Whoosh?"

For 20 minutes, it did appear that all the predictions, all the awe, were justified. It had been said before the game that Tretiak could be the stumbling block, the 'hot goaler' theory being the big topic between semi-finals and final.

Tretiak was certainly hot. He stole in the grand manner which could get a man banished to Siberia forever if there were a legal ground for theft on the ice.

The best collection of shooters ever mustered by Canada hurled 12 shots at him in the first period and Tretiak responded exquisitely. That outpouring of shots was to be almost 50 percent of Canada's total for the evening and, retrospectively, the concensus following the game was that this was the make or break testing ground of the match.

Tretiak broke Canada's heart and spirit in that display and, buoyed by it, the Soviets came reeling out. They unveiled plays they hadn't used previously in the tournament and had the millions of dollars worth of defencemen and forwards opposing them running around grabbing at shadows.

It was expected to be awesome and it turned out that way, only in a reverse of predictions. Hope glimmered briefly in the second period when it stood at 1-1 (Clarke Gillies) matching a goal by Sergei Shepelev) but, from there on, it was stunning. The Soviets moved ahead 3-1 by the end of 40 minutes and rubbed it in with five, fire-at-will scores in the third.

It was devastating and ranked ahead, even, of the 6-0 shutout administered Team NHL in the final game of the 1979 Challenge Cup.

Tretiak didn't have the same work after the first period, but still required his skill and, on occasion, good fortune, to hold Canada to one goal. However, after he had

supplied the confidence base in the opener, it remained for Shepelev — designated the visitor's secret weapon — to crank up the offence. Coming off a two goal semi-final, he blasted three behind Mike Liut in the money game.

Igor Larionov sank two. Others went to Vladimir Krutov, Vladimir Golikov and Alexandr Skvortsov. Krutov's was definitely salt in the wounds, coming on a shorthanded situation.

In the marathon of presentations following the match, it was a popular but not surprising disclosure that Tretiak had been voted not only star of this game but the outstanding player in the series. The boyish

looking and supremely talented goaler has become a North American favorite and as well known as any NHL superstar.

Other awards included a $10,000 ring to Mike Bossy as Canada's outstanding player in the tournament and the Guenther Sabetzki Award (he's president of the IIHF) to Guy Lafleur as the Canadian player best exemplifying what international hockey is all about.

However, the Canadians accepting awards (Marcel Dionne also was given one as Canada's most frequent performer in international play) understandably didn't exhibit the usual enthusiasm for such baubles.

The big one had gotten away.

4

Statistics:
Photo Credits

Final Canada Cup Statistics — 1981
by Ron Andrews, NHL

Combined Standings of Playoff Teams

Team	Games	Won	Lost	Tied	Goals For	Goals Against	Points
Soviet Union	7	5	1	1	32	15	11
Canada	7	5	1	1	37	22	11
Czechoslovakia	6	2	2	2	22	17	6
United States	6	2	3	1	18	23	5

Semi-Final Scores

Friday, Sept. 11	at Ottawa	Soviet Union	4	Czechoslovakia	1
	at Montreal	Canada	4	United States	1

Final Game Score

Sunday, Sept. 13	at Montreal	Soviet Union	8	Canada	1

Individual Scoring Leaders
(Figures in brackets for playoff games)

Player	Team	Games	Goals	Assists	Points
Wayne Gretzky	Canada	7 (2)	5 (0)	7 (1)	12 (1)
Mike Bossy	Canada	7 (2)	8 (2)	3 (1)	11 (3)
Bryan Trottier	Canada	7 (2)	3 (0)	8 (3)	11 (3)
Guy Lafleur	Canada	7 (2)	2 (0)	9 (1)	11 (1)
Alexei Kasatonov	Soviet Union	7 (2)	1 (0)	10 (3)	11 (3)
Gilbert Perreault	Canada	4	3	6	9
Sergei Makarov	Soviet Union	7 (2)	3 (0)	6 (2)	9 (2)
Sergei Shepelev	Soviet Union	7 (2)	6 (5)	2 (1)	8 (6)
Vladimir Krutov	Soviet Union	7 (2)	4 (1)	4 (1)	8 (2)
Vyatcheslav Fetisov	Soviet Union	7 (2)	1 (0)	7 (2)	8 (2)
Clark Gillies	Canada	7 (2)	2 (1)	5 (0)	7 (1)
Denis Potvin	Canada	7 (2)	2 (0)	5 (1)	7 (1)

Penalty Minutes, Power-Play and Penalty-Killing Statistics for Playoff Teams
(Figures in brackets for playoff games)

Team	Games	PIM	Average	ADV	PPG	%	T.S.	PPGA	%	SHG	SHGA
USSR	7 (2)	92 (24)	13.1 (12)	31 (8)	12 (3)	38.7 (37.5)	32 (9)	2 (1)	93.8 (88.9)	3 (1)	0
CZECH	6 (1)	71 (10)	11.8 (10)	30 (5)	6 (1)	20.0 (20.0)	29 (4)	3 (1)	89.7 (75.0)	1 (0)	1 (0)
CAN	7 (2)	76 (26)	10.9 (13)	27 (7)	3 (0)	11.1 (00.0)	32 (10)	7 (3)	78.1 (70.0)	1 (0)	1 (1)
USA	6 (1)	62 (8)	10.3 (8)	27 (6)	4 (1)	14.8 (16.7)	25 (3)	2 (0)	92.0 (100.0)	0	1 (0)

Goaltending Statistics for Playoff Teams
(Figures in brackets for playoff games)

Goaltender	Team	GPI	Minutes	GA	SO	Average	Won	Lost	Tied
Tretiak	USSR	6 (2)	360 (120)	8 (2)	0	1.33 (1.00)	5 (2)	0	1 (0)
Myshkin	USSR	1	60	7	0	7.00	0	1	0
USSR TOTALS		7 (2)	420 (120)	15 (2)	0	2.14 (1.00)	5 (2)	1 (0)	1 (0)
Lang	CZECH	6 (1)	341 (60)	15 (4)	0	2.64 (4.00)	2 (0)	2	2 (0)
Kralik	CZECH	1	19	2	0	6.32	0	1	0
CZECH TOTALS		6 (1)	360 (360)	17 (4)	0	2.83 (4.00)	2 (0)	2 (1)	2 (0)
Edwards	CAN	1	60	3	0	3.00	1	0	1
Liut	CAN	6 (2)	360 (120)	19 (9)	1 (0)	3.17 (4.50)	4 (1)	1 (1)	1 (0)
CAN TOTALS		7 (2)	420 (120)	22 (9)	1 (0)	3.14 (4.50)	5 (1)	1 (1)	1 (0)
Esposito	USA	5 (1)	300 (60)	19 (4)	0	3.80 (4.00)	2 (0)	3 (1)	1
Baker	USA	1	60	4	0	4.00	0	0	1
USA TOTALS		6 (1)	360 (60)	23 (4)	0	3.83 (4.00)	2 (0)	3 (1)	1 (0)

Summary of Shots on Goal for Playoff Teams

(Figures in brackets for playoff games)

Team	Games	Shots For	Average	Shots Against	Average
Canada	7 (2)	227 (50)	32.4 (25)	166 (43)	23.7 (21.5)
Czechoslovakia	6 (1)	180 (27)	31.5 (27)	148 (24)	24.7 (24)
Soviet Union	7 (2)	187 (50)	26.7 (25)	184 (54)	26.3 (27)
United States	6 (1)	168 (17)	28.0 (17)	170 (23)	28.3 (23)

Total Game-Winning, Power-Play & Shorthand Goals for Players of Playoff Teams

(Figures in brackets for playoff games)

Game-Winning Goals

Mike Bossy	Canada	3 (1)
Vladimir Golikov	Soviet Union	1 (1)
Sergei Shepelev	Soviet Union	1 (1)

Power-Play Goals

Sergei Shepelev	Soviet Union	2 (2)
Igor Larionov	Soviet Union	2 (1)
Jiri Lala	Czechoslovakia	2 (1)
Mike Eaves	United States	1 (1)

Shorthand Goals

Vladimir Krutov	Soviet Union	1 (1)

Individual Leaders in Various Categories

Most Goals — Mike Bossy, Canada   8.
Most Assists — Alexei Kasatonov, Soviet Union   10.
Most Points — Wayne Gretzky, Canada   12 (5 goals, 7 assists).
Most Penalty Minutes — Denis Potvin, Canada   12.
Most Shots on Goal — Mike Bossy, Canada   30.
Best Goaltending Average — Vladislav Tretiak, Soviet Union   1.33 (6 games).

Summary of Round-Robin Portion of Canada Cup 1981
Standings

Country	Games	Won	Lost	Tied	For	Against	Points
Canada	5	4	0	1	32	13	9
Soviet Union	5	3	1	1	20	13	7
Czechoslovakia	5	2	1	2	21	13	6
United States	5	2	2	1	17	19	5
Sweden	5	1	4	0	13	20	2
Finland	5	0	4	1	6	31	1

Results of Games

Tuesday, Sept. 1	at Edmonton	United States	3	Sweden	1
	at Winnipeg	Czechoslovakia	1	Soviet Union	1
	at Edmonton	Canada	9	Finland	0
Thursday, Sept. 3	at Edmonton	Czechoslovakia	7	Finland	1
	at Winnipeg	Soviet Union	6	Sweden	3
	at Edmonton	Canada	8	United States	3
Saturday, Sept. 5	at Winnipeg	Sweden	5	Finland	0
	at Edmonton	Soviet Union	4	United States	1
	at Winnipeg	Czechoslovakia	4	Canada	4
Monday, Sept. 7	at Montreal	Canada	4	Sweden	3
	at Winnipeg	Soviet Union	6	Finland	1
	at Montreal	United States	6	Czechoslovakia	2
Wednesday, Sept. 9	at Montreal	Finland	4	United States	4
	at Ottawa	Czechoslovakia	7	Sweden	1
	at Montreal	Canada	7	Soviet Union	3

Individual Scoring Leaders

Player	Team	Games	Goals	Assists	Points
Wayne Gretzky	Canada	5	5	6	11
Guy Lafleur	Canada	5	2	8	10
Gilbert Perreault	Canada	4	3	6	9
Mike Bossy	Canada	5	6	2	8
Bryan Trottier	Canada	5	3	5	8
Alexei Kasatonov	Soviet Union	5	1	7	8
Sergei Makarov	Soviet Union	5	3	4	7
Anders Hedberg	Sweden	5	1	2	6
Jiri Dudacek	Czechoslovakia	5	4	2	6
Vladimir Krutov	Soviet Union	5	3	3	6
Denis Potvin	Canada	5	2	4	6
Clark Gillies	Canada	5	1	5	6
Danny Gare	Canada	5	1	5	6
Steve Christoff	United States	5	1	5	6
Vyatcheslav Fetisov	Soviet Union	5	1	5	6

Statistics for Round-Robin Portion of Canada Cup 1981
Goaltending Statistics
(Figures in brackets for playoff games)

Goaltender	Country	GPI	Minutes	GA	SO	Average	ENG	Won	Lost	Tied
Liut	Canada	4	240	10	1	2.50	0	3	0	1
Edwards	Canada	1	60	3	0	3.00	0	1	0	0
CANADA TOTALS		5	300	12	1	2.60	0	4	0	1
Lang	Czech	5	281	11	0	2.35	0	2	1	2
Kralik	Czech	1	19	2	0	6.32	0	0	0	0
CZECH TOTALS		5	300	13	0	2.60	0	2	1	2
Tretiak	USSR	4	240	6	0	1.50	0	3	0	1
Myshkin	USSR	1	19	2	0	6.32	0	0	0	0
CZECH TOTALS		5	300	13	0	2.60	0	3	1	1
Esposito	USA	4	240	15	0	3.75	0	2	2	0
Baker	USA	1	60	4	0	4.00	0	0	0	1
USA TOTALS		5	300	19	0	3.80	0	2	2	1
Lindmark	Sweden	4	208	11	1	3.17	0	1	3	0
Lindbergh	Sweden	2	92	9	0	5.87	0	0	1	0
SWEDEN TOTALS		5	300	20	1	4.00	0	1	4	0
Lassila	Finland	3	180	16	0	5.33	0	0	2	1
Mattsson	Finland	2	120	15	0	7.50	0	0	2	0
FINLAND TOTALS		5	300	31	0	6.20	0	0	4	1

Power-Play and Penalty-Killing Statistics

TEAM	GP	PIM	AVE	ADV	PPG	%	T.S.	PPGA	%	SHG	SHGA
Soviet Union	5	68	13.6	23	9	39.1	23	1	95.7	2	0
Czechoslovakia	5	61	12.2	25	5	20.0	25	2	92.0	1	1
Sweden	5	58	11.6	18	0	00.0	18	6	66.7	0	1
United States	5	54	10.8	21	3	14.3	22	2	90.9	0	1
Canada	5	54	10.0	20	3	15.0	22	4	81.8	1	0
Finland	5	50	9.6	20	0	00.0	17	5	70.6	0	1
TOTALS	15	339	.6	127	20	15.7	127	20	84.3	4	4

Game-Winning Goals

Bossy, Canada	2
Perreault, Canada	1
Dionne, Canada	1
Kasatonov, Soviet Union	1
Zhlutkov, Soviet Union	1
Drodzetski, Soviet Union	1
Christian, United States	1
Talafous, United	1
Lala, Czechoslovakia	1
Dudacek, Czechoslovakia	1
Hedberg, Sweden	1

Power-Play Goals

Bossy, Canada	2
Talafous, United States	2
Makarov, Soviet Union	2
Larinov, Soviet Union	2
Dudacek, Czechoslovakia	2
Lafleur, Canada	1
Kapustin, Soviet Union	1
Kasatonov, Soviet Union	1
Krutov, Soviet Union	1
Fetisov, Soviet Union	1
Shalimov, Soviet Union	1
Dunn, United States	1
Richter, Czechoslovakia	1
Lala, Czechoslovakia	1
Horava, Czechoslovakia	1

Game-Tying Goals

Nova, Czechoslovakia	1
Dudacek, Czechoslovakia	1
Drodzdetski, Soviet Union	1
Gainey, Canada	1
W. Miller, United States	1
Javanainen, Finland	1

Short-Hand Goals

Maltsev, Soviet Union	1
Zhuluktov, Soviet Union	1
Goring, Canada	1
Kokrment, Czechoslovakia	1

Teams' Shots on Goal Totals

Team	Games	For	Average	Against	Average
Canada	5	177	35.4	123	24.6
Czechoslovakia	5	162	32.4	124	24.8
United States	5	151	30.2	147	29.4
Soviet Union	5	137	27.4	130	26.0
Sweden	5	134	26.8	148	29.6
Finland	5	115	23.0	204	40.8
TOTALS	15	876		976	

Individual Statistics
(Figures in brackets for playoff games)
Canada

Player	Games	Goals	Assists	Points	PIM	Shots
Wayne Gretzky, Edmonton	7 (2)	5 (0)	7 (1)	12 (1)	2 (2)	18 (5)
Mike Bossy, N.Y. Islanders	7 (2)	8 (2)	3 (1)	11 (3)	2 (2)	30 (9)
Bryan Trottier, N.Y. Islanders	7 (2)	3 (0)	8 (3)	11 (3)	6	14 (4)
Guy Lafleur, Montreal	7 (2)	2 (0)	9 (1)	11 (1)	0	18 (2)
Gilbert Perreault, Buffalo	4	3	6	9	2	8
Clark Gillies, N.Y. Islanders	7 (2)	2 (1)	5 (0)	7 (1)	8 (2)	12 (2)
Denis Potvin, N.Y. Islanders	7 (2)	2 (0)	5 (1)	7 (1)	12 (6)	20 (2)
Danny Gare, Buffalo	7 (2)	1	5	6	2	11 (1)
Marcel Dionne, Los Angeles	6 (2)	4 (1)	1 (0)	5 (1)	4 (2)	15 (6)
Butch Goring, N.Y. Islanders	7 (2)	3 (0)	2 (1)	5 (1)	4	10 (3)
Raymond Bourque, Boston	7 (2)	1	4	5	6 (2)	12 (0)
Bob Gainey, Montreal	7 (2)	1 (0)	3 (1)	4 (1)	2	8 (1)
Rick Middleton, Boston	7 (2)	1	2	3	0	12 (3)
Ron Guguay, N.Y. Rangers	7 (2)	0	2	2	6 (2)	9 (0)
Brian Engblom, Montreal	5 (2)	1 (1)	0	1 (1)	4 (2)	3 (2)
Ken Linseman, Philadelphia	4 (2)	0	1	1	4 (2)	1 (0)
Craig Hartsburg, Minnesota	7 (2)	0	1	1	6 (4)	12 (7)
Larry Robinson, Montreal	7 (2)	0	1 (1)	1 (1)	2	8 (2)
Paul Reinhart, Calgary	2	0	0	0	2	2
Barry Beck, N.Y. Rangers	7 (2)	0	0	0	2	4 (1)
Mike Luit, St. Louis	6 (2)	0	1	1	0	—
TOURNAMENT TOTALS	6 (2)	37 (5)	66 (10)	103 (15)	76 (26)	227 (50)

Individual Statistics
(Figures in brackets for playoff games)
Czechoslovakia

Player	Games	Goals	Assists	Points	PIM	Shots
Jiri Dudacek, Poldi Kladno	6 (1)	4	2	6	4	16 (5)
Jiri Lala, Dukla Jihlava	6 (1)	4 (1)	2 (0)	6 (1)	0	17 (5)
Jindrich Kokrment, CHZ Litvinov	6 (1)	2	3	5	2	7 (0)
Darius Rusnak, Slovan Bratislava	6 (1)	4	0	4	10 (4)	11 (1)
Pavel Richter, Sparta Praha	3	1	2	3	2	6
Arnold Kadlec, CHZ Litvinov	6 (1)	1	2	3	4	15 (2)
Milan Novy, Poldi Kladno	6 (1)	1	2	3	7	15 (2)
Radoslav Svoboda, Dukla Jihlava	5 (1)	0	3	3	4	13 (4)
Miroslav Dvorak, Budejovice	6 (1)	0	3 (1)	3 (1)	2	8 (1)
Norbert Kral, Budejovice	6 (1)	2	0	2	0	7 (1)
Miloslav Horava, Poldi Kladno	6 (1)	2	0	2	2	20 (0)
Jaroslav Pouzar, Budejovice	6 (1)	1	1	2	4	10 (1)
Milan Chalupa, Dukla Jihlava	6 (1)	0	2	2	4 (4)	6 (0)
Lubomir Penicka, Sparta Praha	6 (1)	0	2	2	2	4 (0)
Dusan Pasek, Slovan Bratislava	6 (1)	0	2	2	2	8 (1)
Stanislav Hajdusek, Sparta Praha	6 (1)	0	1	1	4	9 (2)
Jaroslav Korbela, Budejovice	6 (1)	0	1	1	6	6 (0)
Jan Neliba, Poldi Kladno	2	0	0	0	2	1
Oldrick Valek, Dukla Johlava	3 (1)	0	0	0	4 (2)	4 (0)
Frantisek Cernick, TJ Vitkovice	6 (1)	0	0	0	0	6 (2)
Karel Lang, Zetor Brno	5 (1)	0	0	0	4	—
Bench Minor	—	—	—	—	2	— (0)
CZECHOSLOVAKIA TOTALS	6 (1)	22 (1)	28 (1)	50 (2)	71 (10)	189 (27)

Individual Statistics
Finland

Player	Games	Goals	Assists	Points	PIM	Shots
Matti Hagman, Edmonton Oilers	5	1	2	3	4	4
Risto Siltanen, Edmonton Oilers	5	1	1	2	6	14
Ilkka Sinisalo, Helsinki	5	1	0	1	6	7
Art Javanainen, Assat Pori	5	1	0	1	2	3
Jukka Porvari, Tappara Tampere	5	1	0	1	0	11
Markku Kiimalainen, Karpat Oulu	5	1	0	1	0	8
Tapio Levo, Assat Pori	5	0	1	1	2	6
Pekka Rautakallio, Calgary Flames	5	0	1	1	2	7
Reijo Ruotsalainen, Karpat Oulu	5	0	1	1	2	11
Kari Jalonen, Karpat Oulu	5	0	1	1	4	4
Mikko Leinonen, Karpat Oulu	5	0	1	1	0	9
Jari Kurri, Edmonton Oilers	5	0	1	1	0	8
Jorma Sevon, Tappara Tampere	5	0	1	1	4	4
Juha Huikari, Karpat Oulu	3	0	0	0	4	1
Timo Nummelin, TPS Turku	2	0	0	0	0	0
Raimo Hirvonen, IFK Helsinki	3	0	0	0	2	5
Juha Tuohimaa, Karpat Oulu	3	0	0	0	2	2
Kari Makkonen, Assat Pori	3	0	0	0	0	3
Veli-Pekka Ketola, Assat Pori	5	0	0	0	6	4
Pekka Arbelius, Karpat Oulu	5	0	0	0	2	4
FINLAND TOTALS	5	6	10	16	48	115

Individual Statistics
(Figures in brackets for playoff games)
Soviet Union

Player	Games	Goals	Assists	Points	PIM	Shots
Alexei Kasatonov, Soviet Army	7 (2)	1 (0)	10 (3)	11 (3)	8 (2)	7 (2)
Sergei Makarov, Soviet Army	7 (2)	3 (0)	6 (2)	9 (2)	0	16 (4)
Sergei Shepelev, Soviet Army	7 (2)	6 (5)	2 (1)	8 (6)	4	18 (13)
Vladimir Krutov, Soviet Army	7 (2)	4 (1)	4 (1)	8 (2)	10 (6)	16 (3)
Vyatcheslav Festisov, Soviet Army	7 (2)	1 (0)	7 (2)	8 (2)	10 (2)	9 (1)
Igor Larionov, Soviet Army	7 (2)	4 (2)	1 (0)	5 (2)	8 (2)	0 (2)
Sergei Kapustin, Spartak	6 (2)	2 (0)	2 (1)	4 (1)	6 (2)	13 (6)
Nikolai Drozdetski, Soviet Army	7 (2)	2	2	4	2	10 (1)
Victor Shalimov, Spartak	7 (2)	2 (1)	2 (1)	4 (2)	2	10 (2)
Vladimir Golikov, Dynamo	7 (2)	3 (2)	0	3 (2)	4	10 (3)
Victor Zhluktov, Soviet Army	7 (2)	2	0	2	4 (2)	19 (3)
Alexander Maltsev, Dynamo	4	1	1	2	0	3
Vasily Pervukhin, Dynamo	6 (2)	0	2 (1)	2 (1)	6	3 (2)
Sergei Babinov, Soviet Army	7 (2)	0	2	2	0	7 (0)
Alexander Skovortsov, Torpedo	7 (2)	1 (1)	0	1 (1)	4 (4)	12 (1)
Vladimir Zubkov, Soviet Army	2	0	1	1	4	1
Irek Gimaev, Soviet Army	4 (2)	0	1 (1)	1 (1)	4 (2)	7 (4)
Valery Vasiliev, Dynamo	6 (2)	0	1 (1)	1 (1)	4	5 (1)
Zinetula Bilyaletdinov, Dynamo	7 (2)	0	1 (1)	1 (1)	8 (2)	6 (1)
Andrei Khomutov, Soviet Army	7 (2)	0	0	0	2	5 (1)
Vladislav Tretiak, Soviet Army	6 (2)	0	0	0	2	—
TOURNAMENT TOTALS	6 (2)	32 (12)	45 (15)	77 (27)	92	187 (50)

Individual Statistics
Sweden

Player	Games	Goals	Assists	Points	PIM	Shots
Anders Hedberg, N.Y. Rangers	5	4	2	6	0	17
Anders Kallur, N.Y. Islanders	5	3	1	4	0	15
Lars Molin, MoDo AIK	5	2	2	4	0	7
Ulf Nilsson, N.Y. Rangers	4	1	2	3	2	2
Thomas Gradin, Vancouver Canucks	5	1	2	3	4	9
Anders Haakansson, AIK Stockholm	5	1	1	2	4	9
Kent Nilsson, Calgary Flames	5	0	2	2	4	6
Peter Helander, Skelleftea IF	5	0	2	2	8	7
Borje Salming, Toronto Maple Leafs	5	0	2	2	10	10
Patrik Sundstroem, Bjoerkioeven IF	5	0	2	2	4	8
Bengt Lundholm, Stockholm AIK	5	1	0	1	2	11
Tomas Jonsson, MoDo AIK	2	0	1	1	4	3
Kent-Erik Andersson, Minnesota	5	0	1	1	0	5
Lars Lindgren, Vancouver Canucks	5	0	1	1	6	9
Jan Erixon, Skelleftea IF	2	0	0	0	0	1
Ulf Isaksson, Philadelphia	1	0	0	0	0	0
Thomas Eriksson, Philadelphia	3	0	0	0	0	3
Thomas Steen, Winnipeg Jets	3	0	0	0	2	3
Mats Waltin, Djurgardens IF	5	0	0	0	2	2
Jorgen Pettersson, St. Louis	5	0	0	0	0	7
Stefan Persson, N.Y. Islanders	5	0	0	0	2	0
Peter Lindmark, Timraa IK	3	0	1	1	2	0
Bench Minor	—	—	—	—	2	—
TOTALS	5	13	22	35	58	134

Individual Statistics
(Figures in brackets for playoff games)
United States

Player	Games	Goals	Assists	Points	PIM	Shots
Mike Eaves, Minnesota	6 (1)	3 (1)	3 (0)	6 (1)	4	13 (1)
Steve Christoff, Minnesota	6 (1)	1	5	6	4	12 (1)
Neal Broten, Minnesota	6 (1)	3	2	5	0	17 (3)
Dean Talafous, N.Y. Rangers	6 (1)	3	2	5	0	12 (1)
Mike O'Connell, Boston	4 (1)	1	3	4	2	11 (1)
Richie Dunn, Buffalo	6 (1)	1 (0)	3 (1)	4 (1)	4 (4)	10 (0)
Mark Johnson, Pittsburgh	6 (1)	1 (0)	3 (1)	4 (1)	2	14 (0)
Mark Howe, Hartford	6 (1)	0	4	4	2	11 (1)
Warren Miller, Hartford	6 (1)	2	0	2	2 (2)	8 (0)
Reed Larson, Detroit	5 (1)	1	1	2	4	6 (1)
Tom Gorence, Philadelphia	6 (1)	1	1	2	2	8 (2)
Dave Christian, Winnipeg	6 (1)	1	0	1	4	8 (1)
Dave Langevin, N.Y. Islanders	6 (1)	0	1	1	8 (2)	7 (0)
Rod Langway, Montreal	6 (1)	0	1	1	8	12 (3)
Bob Miller, Colorado	6 (1)	0	1	1	6	10 (0)
Bill Baker, Colorado	1	0	0	0	0	0
Tom Younghans, Minnesota	4 (1)	0	0	0	0	1 (1)
Robbie Ftorek, Quebec	4	0	0	0	0	1
Ken Morrow, N.Y. Islanders	6 (1)	0	0	0	6	5 (1)
Rob McClanahan, Buffalo	6 (1)	0	0	0	2	2 (0)
Bench Minor	—	—	—	—	23 (0)	—
UNITED STATES TOTALS	6 (1)	18 (1)	30 (2)	48 (3)	62 (8)	168 (17)

Photo Credits

Dave Bonner
37, 39, 46

Bill Brennan
34, 35, 36, 38, 42,
43, 44, 45, 48, 68 (top),
71, 77, 92, 93, 96

Denis Brodeur
13, 14, 16, 19, 20,
21, 22, 24, 27, 28,
30, 31, 33, 40, 47,
65, 66, 67, 68, 69, 70, 72, 74 (right),
74 (top), 75, 76, 78,
79, 80, 81, 82, 83,
84, 85, 86, 87, 88,
89, 94, 95, 99, 100,
101, 102, 103, 104,
105, 106, 107, 108,
109, 110, 111

Murray Mosher
74 (left), 90, 91

Paul Taillfer
73, 97, 98